Heinemann Games Series

WORD GAMES WITH ENGLISH

TEACHER'S RESOURCE BOOK 2

DEIRDRE HOWARD-WILLIAMS & CYNTHIA HERD

REVISED EDITION IN THREE LEVELS

Heinemann Games Series

Titles in this series include:

TEACHER'S RESOURCE BOOKS		CLASS BOOKS	
Play Games with English 1	0 435 25016 7	Play Games with English 1	0 435 28060 0
Play Games with English 2	0 435 25017 5	Play Games with English 2	0 435 28062 7
Play Games with English 3	0 435 25018 3		
Word Games with English 1	0 435 25088 4	Word Games with English 1	0 435 28380 4
Word Games with English 2	0 435 25089 2	Word Games with English 2	0 435 28381 2
Word Games with English 3	0 435 25090 6	Word Games with English 3	0 435 28382 0
		Word Games with English Plus	0 435 28379 0
English Puzzles 1	0 435 25084 1	English Puzzles 1	0 435 28280 8
English Puzzles 2	0 435 25085 X	English Puzzles 2	0 435 28281 6
English Puzzles 3	0 435 25086 8	English Puzzles 3	0 435 28282 4
		English Puzzles 4	0 435 28283 2

Heinemann English Language Teaching
A division of Heinemann Publishers (Oxford) Ltd
Halley Court, Jordan Hill, Oxford OX2 8EJ

OXFORD MADRID ATHENS PARIS FLORENCE PRAGUE SÃO PAULO
CHICAGO MELBOURNE AUCKLAND SINGAPORE TOKYO GABORONE
JOHANNESBURG PORTSMOUTH (NH) IBADAN

ISBN 0 435 25089 2

© Deirdre Howard-Williams and Cynthia Herd 1994
First published 1994

PERMISSION TO COPY

The material in this book is copyright. However, the publisher grants permission for copies of pages to be made without fee on those pages marked with the PHOTOCOPIABLE symbol.

Private purchasers may make copies for their own use or for use by classes of which they are in charge; school purchasers may make copies for use within and by the staff and students of the school only. This permission does not extend to additional schools or branches of an institution, who should purchase a separate master copy of the book for their own use.

For copying in any other circumstances, prior permission in writing must be obtained from Heinemann Publishers (Oxford) Ltd.

Illustrated by
Tony Kenyon and Trevor Waugh

Cover designed by Martin Cox

Teacher's pages designed and typeset by VAP

Dedicated to the memory of Richard Astley Herd and Lilian Irene Butterly

Printed and bound in Great Britain by
Thomson Litho Limited, East Kilbride, Scotland.

93 94 95 96 97 98 10 9 8 7 6 5 4 3 2 1

Contents

N.B. Each game in this list has a brief description given below it. Where there are no descriptions indicating the type of vocabulary used, e.g. doubles, abbreviations etc, the games are of mixed vocabulary, or are self-explanatory.

Title	Page
Introduction	4
OO and EE words	6
Masculine and Feminine	7
Clothes	8
Odd One Out 1	9
Money *Word Square*	10
At the Theatre	11
What Would You Say? *Everyday Phrases*	12
Abbreviations	13
Emergency *Services*	14
Crossword 1 *Punctuation and Writing*	15
Christmas Shopping *Shop Departments*	16
Prepositions 1 *Expressions with "at"*	18
Person or Thing *Words which end in -er*	19
Nationalities *Word Square*	20
Word Families	21
Thieves *What they Damage/Use/Find*	22
Help in the Home *Housework Verbs*	23
Make a Choice *Descriptions, Right or Wrong?*	24
Shopping Centre *Shops*	25
Doubles 1	26
Thank You *In Different Situations*	27
Work for Us! *Job Advertisements*	28
Odd One Out 2	29
Prepositions 2 *Expressions with "in"*	30
Travel Quiz *Holiday Vocabulary*	31
Where Does It Go? *Objects for Storing/Keeping Things In*	32
Crossword 2 *Entertainment*	33
Prefixes & Suffixes	34
In the Press *Extracts from a Newspaper*	35
Books *Study Subjects*	36
The Word Snake *Transport and Movement*	37
Time Off *Objects for Leisure Activities*	38
The Word Snail *The Countryside*	39
Words Easily Confused	40
Doubles 2	41
Words Beginning With CAR-	42
Odd One Out 3 *Adjectives*	43
Make and Do	44
Words and Meanings *Words with More than One Meaning*	45
The Wastepaper Basket *Office Items*	46
The Name Game *Boys' and Girls' Names*	47
Cross It Out	48
What's on the Menu?	49
Connections	50
The Family Tree *Relations*	51
Words Ending in -TION	52
The S Connection *Nouns which exist only in the plural*	53
Collectives *Collective Nouns*	54
Complaints *Result of Something Wrong*	55
Language Functions *Describing Utterances*	56
Proverbs	58
Doubles 3	59
The Weather Forecast *Word Square*	60
Purchases *Product Information*	61
Festivals and Feast Days	62
Body Talk *Compound Words*	63
Odd One Out 4 *The Countryside*	64
Verb Pieces *Verb with Preposition*	65
Answers	66
Word List	73

WORD GAMES WITH ENGLISH
Teacher's Introduction

WORD GAMES WITH ENGLISH is a series of three books of carefully graded language activities designed to stimulate learners to practise, activate and extend their English vocabulary.

Each book contains 60 games on photocopiable students' pages plus a full answer key and word list. Each page is highly visual with the words contextualised and their meanings made clear by the illustrations.

Why use games?

Games are an extremely effective way of motivating students in a classroom. Language teachers throughout history have interspersed their grammar or course material with what often seem like lighthearted games, but they do actually touch the language directly and are challenging. And, most importantly perhaps, games are fun!

These resource books are designed to test English vocabulary under the guise of motivating classroom entertainment. You may choose to use them occasionally alongside a standard course or as the basis of a set of needs-orientated one-shot lessons. Each activity could form the core 20 minutes of a vocabulary lesson or maybe the final 20 minutes of a more formal coursebook lesson. For your own reference we have indexed the vocabulary at the back to the page where it occurs.

BOOK 1 is for beginners and post-beginners and contains over 1000 lexical items, allowing the learner to deal with most everyday situations and providing a sound basis for further study. The vocabulary concentrates on the most essential topic areas: personal and family/free time and entertainment/travel/food and drink etc and there is build-in revision and recycling of certain lexical items in different contexts.

BOOK 2 is for intermediate learners who have a general vocabulary of everyday words. By concentrating on a wide variety of up-to-date topics and by developing an awareness of language forms (word building/prefixes and suffixes/prepositional phrases/abbreviations etc) the games enrich and extend this basic vocabulary and enable the learner to understand and express a wider variety of ideas.

BOOK 3 is designed for upper-intermediate learners and corresponds to the standard demanded for the University of Cambridge First Certificate in English, where students are expected to have a good level of general English vocabulary in the 4000 to 5000 word range. Extensive use has been made of authentic materials, such as travel brochures, information booklets and newspapers and special practice has been given in collocation, lexical choice and appropriacy.

Using WORD GAMES WITH ENGLISH in the Classroom

You will find many different types of word games in this book, including crosswords, synonyms, word squares etc and your students will be asked to do different things such as match words and pictures, choose the correct word and fill in blanks.

If you work through the games in order you will find plenty of variety to sustain interest and motivation and your students will benefit from the graded progression and recycling of vocabulary.

However, flexibility is a key feature of WORD GAMES WITH ENGLISH and you may prefer to select games to fill lexical gaps and provide additional practice in a way that will complement other language course material in use. The word list can be used to see where specific vocabulary occurs to enable you to select games of particular interest and relevance to your students' needs.

Students will usually be able to write their answers on the page itself although some games may need extra paper.

Start by making sure that all the students understand exactly what to do. An example is always given so look at this closely. If necessary, do another example with the whole class.

Then the game can either be set for homework to be corrected in a later lesson or can be played in the classroom. Students can work

- (i) individually
- (ii) in pairs
- (iii) in small groups/teams.

You can choose how you do the games, depending on the size of your class and the type of teaching situation. However two ideas are worth bearing in mind.

Generally, those games where the words are all given and then have to be matched either with the correct picture or with another word work well if students try to do as much as they can individually and then compare their work with that of another student, discussing any differences and trying to complete the game between them.

Those games that involve the students in finding the words themselves from a variety of prompts (e.g. crosswords) are often best done in small groups/teams so that knowledge can be pooled and team-work and competition can help them to come up with the answers.

While they are working on the games, walk round the classroom to give help and make suggestions where necessary. Encourage everyone to use English as far as possible and not to give up too easily!

Correction can be done in a variety of ways.

(i) Individual students can exchange their work and correct one another's answers.

(ii) You can call on individual students to come out to the front of the class and say/write their answers for the others to comment on.

(iii) You can ask students (individuals or groups) for their answers and write these on the board.

(iv) You can take the pages in and correct them yourself, giving them back in a later lesson and discussing any problems.

Encourage students to keep the games afterwards as a record and to make a note of all the new vocabulary they have learnt.

oo and ee

Look at this picture.
Can you find 11 words with double o 'OO' and 8 with double e 'EE'?

For example: b<u>oo</u>ts, sl<u>ee</u>ves

MASCULINE and FEMININE

What is the feminine of these words?

For example:

1. male _female_
2. actor _____
3. uncle _____
4. bull _____
5. steward _____
6. king _____
7. hero _____

And what is the masculine of these words?

For example:

8. lioness _lion_
9. Englishwoman _____
10. mistress _____
11. wife _____
12. waitress _____
13. niece _____
14. lady _____

Clothes

Can you name and describe the clothes these people are wearing?
Put the correct word from list A with the correct description from list B.

For example:
1. A large handkerchief

A	B
1. handkerchief	fur
2. T-shirt	patterned
3. bra	plastic
4. sweater	dark
5. raincoat	short-sleeved
6. tie	collarless
7. belt	silk
8. shirt	plain
9. suit	child's
10. gloves	large

© Deirdre Howard-Williams and Cynthia Herd 1994
HEINEMANN ENGLISH LANGUAGE TEACHING

Odd One OUT 1

Look at these groups of words.
Which word does not fit?

For example:

1. SMILE
KISS
TASTE
~~LISTEN~~

2. STADIUM
GROUND
FIELD
TEAM

3. STRING
SOAP
TOWEL
RAZOR

4. PIG
HORSE
SHEEP
BEEF

5. MEANING
INCORRECT
MISTAKE
WRONG

6. CELLAR
LAVATORY
ROOF
STAIRS

MONEY

In this word square there are 15 hidden words, all connected with money matters. The words are horizontal ⬭, vertical ⬭, or diagonal ⬭.

For example:

A	C	B	P	R	I	C	E	C	T
T	O	U	D	R	E	Z	Y	V	A
R	I	D	R	C	O	S	T	E	X
E	N	P	F	R	G	F	H	Q	A
C	H	E	Q	U	E	B	I	L	L
E	W	U	W	I	E	N	L	T	X
I	A	C	A	S	H	A	C	F	Y
P	G	J	S	A	L	A	R	Y	M
T	E	D	I	S	C	O	U	N	T

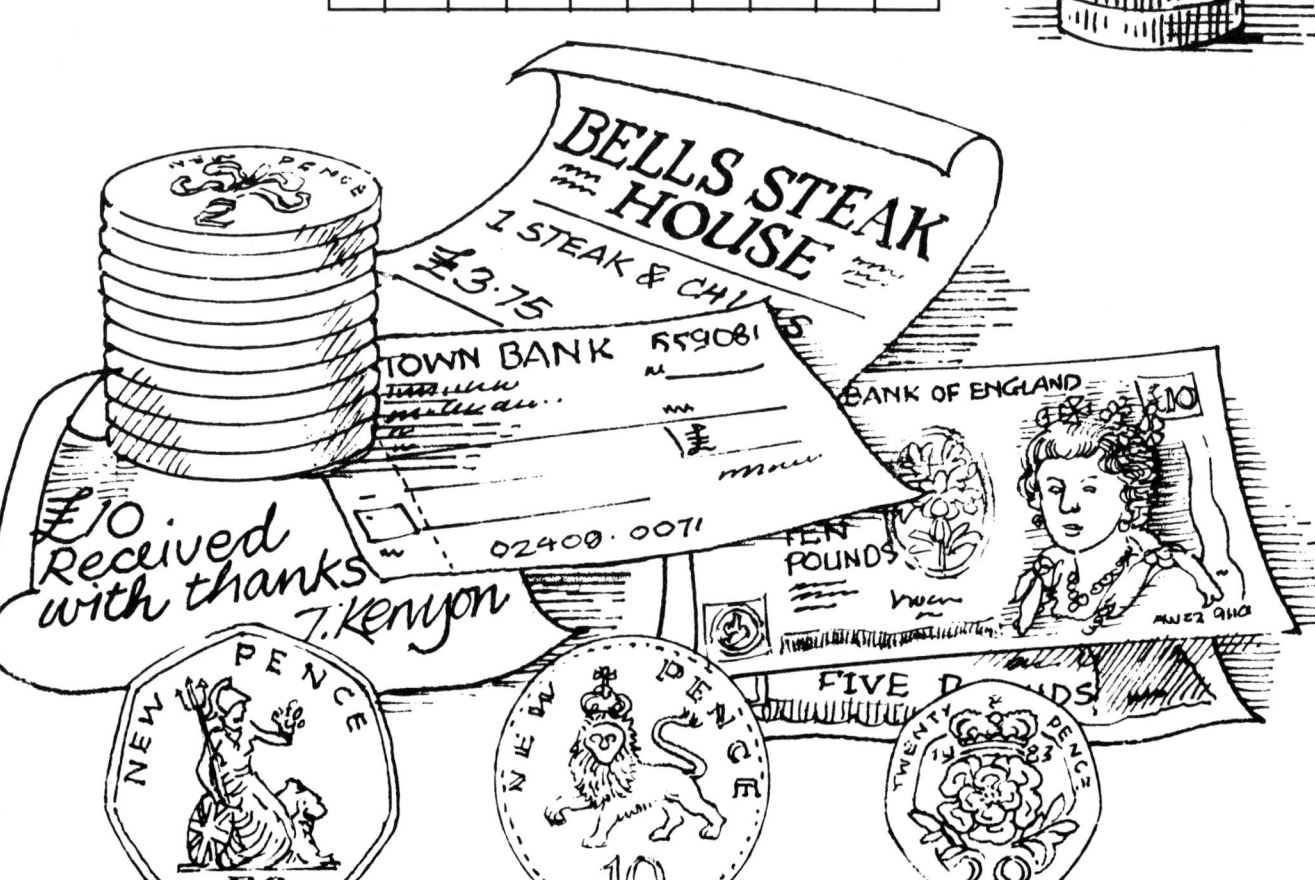

PHOTOCOPIABLE

© Deirdre Howard-Williams and Cynthia Herd 1994
HEINEMANN ENGLISH LANGUAGE TEACHING

AT THE THEATRE

Can you find your way in an English theatre?

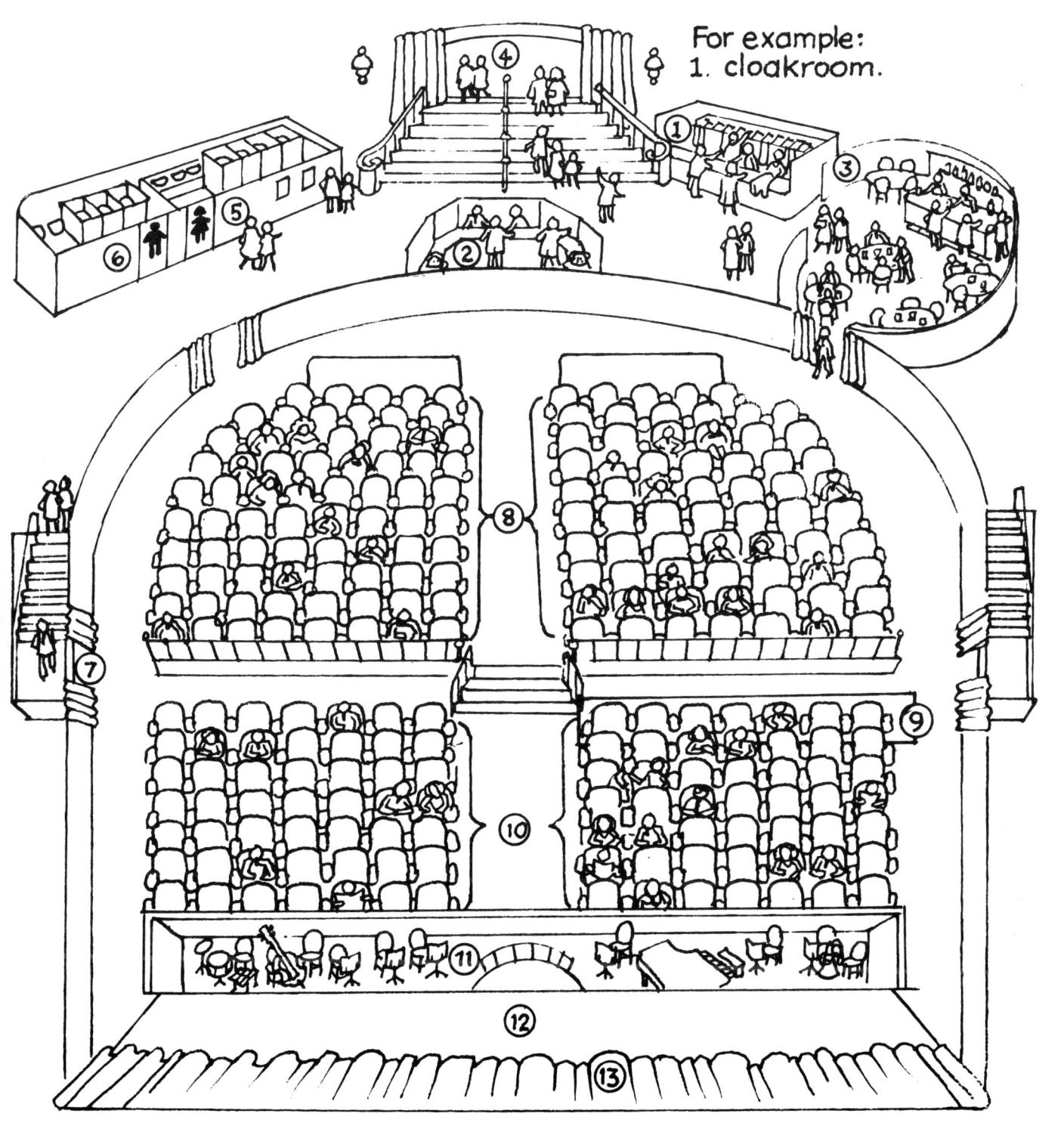

For example:
1. cloakroom.

cloakroom   row   orchestra   stage   emergency exit   bar   entrance
front seats   ladies   back seats   gents   booking office   curtain

© Deirdre Howard-Williams and Cynthia Herd 1994
HEINEMANN ENGLISH LANGUAGE TEACHING

What Would You Say?

Look at these everyday situations. Do you know what to say?

For example: 1. What's the matter?

What's the matter?   Cheerio.   Good Luck.   That's a pity.   Excuse me.
Mind out!   May I introduce you to Peter Brown?   What a surprise!
Sorry.   Cheers.   No thank you.   How do you do?

ABBREVIATIONS

Can you fill in the correct abbreviations?

For example:

Information

Opposite

Please reply

In other words (that is)

Christmas

January

Member of Parliament

Post Office

Long-playing (record)

President

In the centre box you now have 2 words.
Do you know the abbreviation for these 2 words?

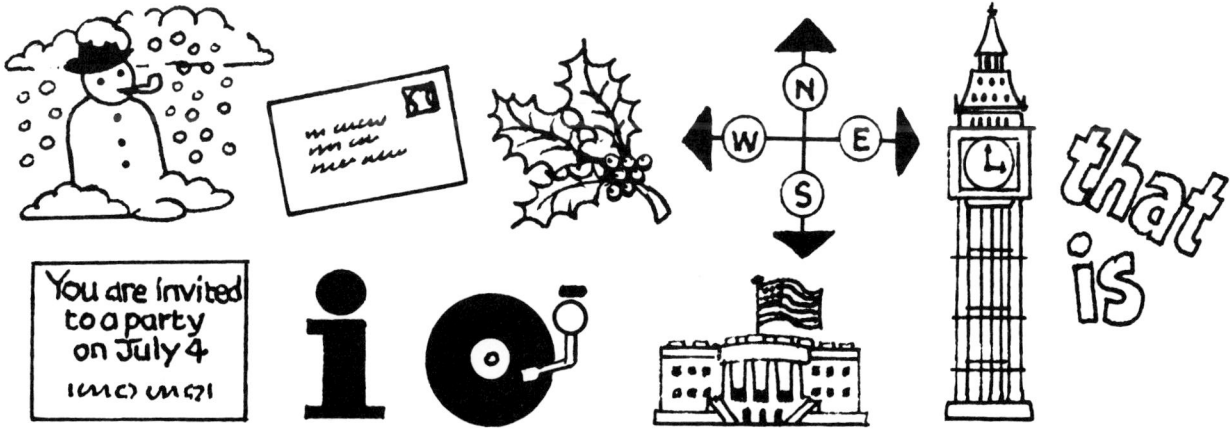

© Deirdre Howard-Williams and Cynthia Herd 1994
HEINEMANN ENGLISH LANGUAGE TEACHING

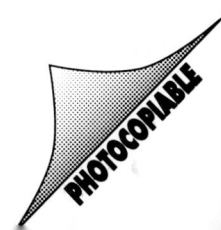

EMERGENCY

Help! These 8 people have problems. What services do they need? Can you find the solutions in the box?

1. My pet is ill. — For example: (A) Vet
2. My money has been stolen.
3. I've broken my leg!
4. FIRE! FIRE!
5. My light doesn't work.
6. My dress is dirty.
7. My car has broken down.
8. I've lost my glasses.

A, B, C, D, E, F, G, H

vet   optician   police   dry cleaner   mechanic
ambulance   fire service   electrician

14

© Deirdre Howard-Williams and Cynthia Herd 1994
HEINEMANN ENGLISH LANGUAGE TEACHING

CROSSWORD 1

All the answers are connected with **punctuation** and **writing**.

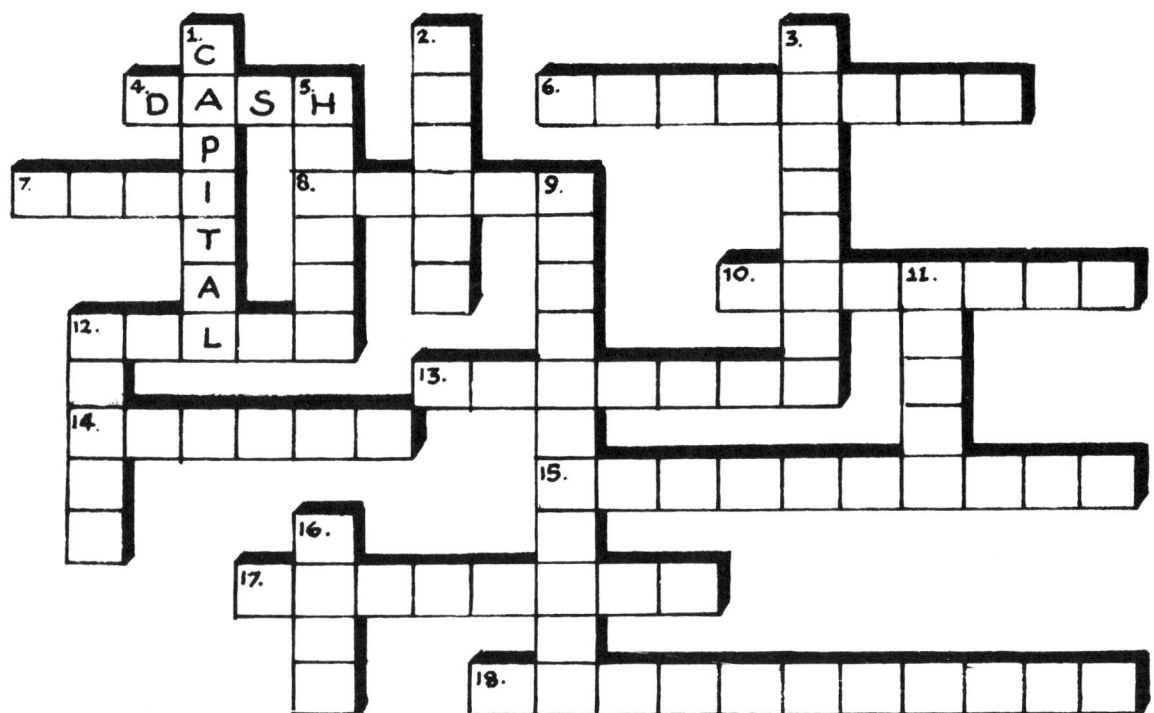

ACROSS →

4. —
6. ⁶⁶ ⁹⁹ (_____ commas)
7. ; (_____ colon)
8. • • •
10. LATEST ←
12. :
13. ~~the~~ the
14. |← →|
15. it ' s
17. ? (_____ mark)
18. the

DOWN ↓

1. <u>E</u>nglish (_____ letter)
2. (columns of text)
3. ( )
5. - week-end
9. ! (_____ mark)
11. " (2 tins of beans, " " " carrots)
12. ,
16. • (_____ stop)

© Deirdre Howard-Williams and Cynthia Herd 1994
HEINEMANN ENGLISH LANGUAGE TEACHING

CHRISTMAS

Look at Susan's Christmas presents. Who are they for?
Put the correct names on her list.

Christmas list
spade — Bill
teddy bear
fridge
shirt
shoes
pack of cards
record
purse
suitcase
hammer
cupboard
football
Christmas cake

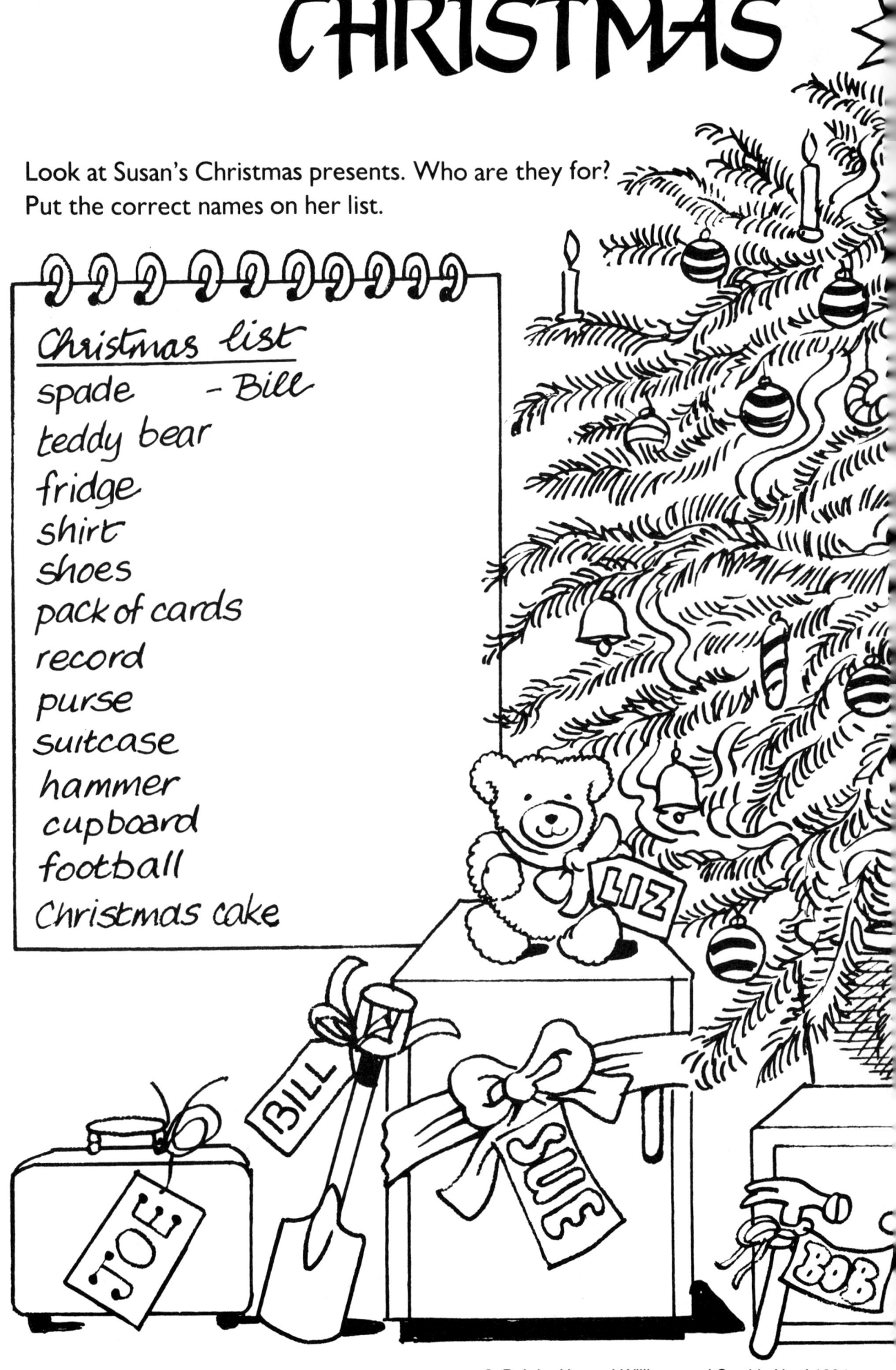

SHOPPING

Susan bought all her Christmas presents in one big shop.
Which departments did she go to?

SUPER SHOP

DEPARTMENTS

Children's

Do-it-Yourself

Food

Footwear

Furniture

Games

Gardening

Kitchen

Luggage

Men's

Music

Sports

Women's Leather Goods

teddy bear

© Deirdre Howard-Williams and Cynthia Herd 1994
HEINEMANN ENGLISH LANGUAGE TEACHING

PREPOSITIONS 1

Here are 10 very common expressions with **at**. Do you know them all?

For example: 1. at university

university   sea   full speed   home   work
school   war   peace   church   breakfast

Person or Thing?

Here are 20 words which end in **-er**.
Which of them is a person and which is a thing?
Make 2 lists.

For example:

Person	Thing
driver	lighter

LIGHTER
DRIVER
SAUCER
PASSENGER
PHOTOGRAPHER

COOKER
SHOWER
PLAYER
EMPLOYER
TRAVELLER

SCOOTER
FOREIGNER
LABOURER
TYPEWRITER
MEMBER

GROCER
INTERVIEWER
NOTEPAPER
DANCER
FARMER

© Deirdre Howard-Williams and Cynthia Herd 1994
HEINEMANN ENGLISH LANGUAGE TEACHING

NATIONALITIES

In this word square there are 12 hidden words. They are all different nationalities.
The words are horizontal ⌒ vertical ◯ or diagonal ⬭
The hats will help you.

For example: chinese

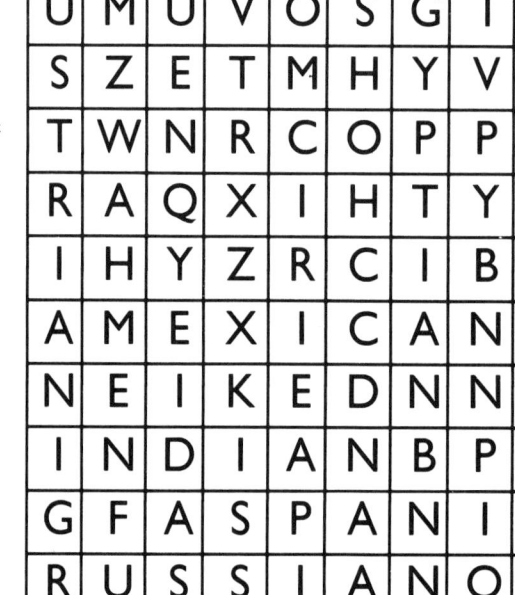

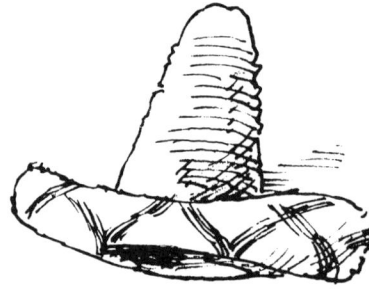

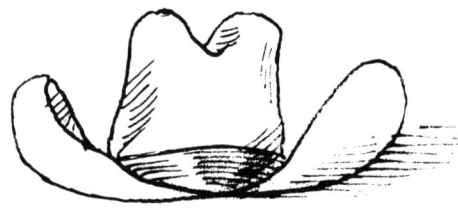

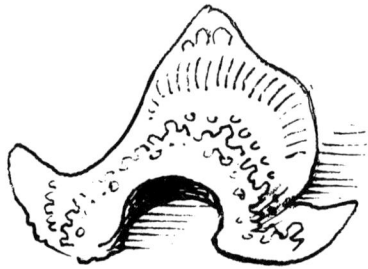

S	C	O	T	T	I	S	H	V	S
A	D	F	P	F	R	E	N	C	H
U	M	U	V	O	S	G	T	L	B
S	Z	E	T	M	H	Y	V	U	R
T	W	N	R	C	O	P	P	S	I
R	A	Q	X	I	H	T	Y	C	T
I	H	Y	Z	R	C	I	B	H	I
A	M	E	X	I	C	A	N	I	S
N	E	I	K	E	D	N	N	N	H
I	N	D	I	A	N	B	P	E	M
G	F	A	S	P	A	N	I	S	H
R	U	S	S	I	A	N	O	E	N

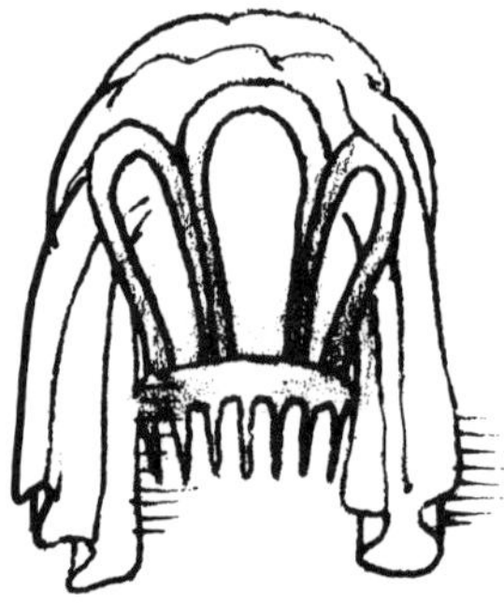

© Deirdre Howard-Williams and Cynthia Herd 1994
HEINEMANN ENGLISH LANGUAGE TEACHING

Word Families

Can you put these words into 5 different subject groups? There are 4 words in each.

Atlantic   buffet   North Sea   classical   Africa   water   Pacific   rock   canteen   gas   snack bar   pop   Australasia   pub   jazz   Europe   phone   Mediterranean   Asia   electricity

1.

For example:
Atlantic
_____
_____
_____

2.

_____
_____
_____
_____

3.

_____
_____
_____
_____

4.

_____
_____
_____
_____

5.

_____
_____
_____
_____

THIEVES

Look at the pictures and answer the questions.

What did the thieves damage? What did the thieves use?
For example:
1. hedge   drainpipe   2. _____ _____

hedge   drainpipe   picture   washing line   torch   blood
jewellery   window   dustbin   television aerial   clock
ladder   footprints   handbag   bricks   scarf

What did the thieves find?   What did the detective find?

3. _____ _____   4. _____ _____

PHOTOCOPIABLE

© Deirdre Howard-Williams and Cynthia Herd 1994
HEINEMANN ENGLISH LANGUAGE TEACHING

Help in the Home

Mrs. Brown is talking to her au pair girl Marie and asking her to do different things in the house.
Look at the pictures and tell Marie what to do.

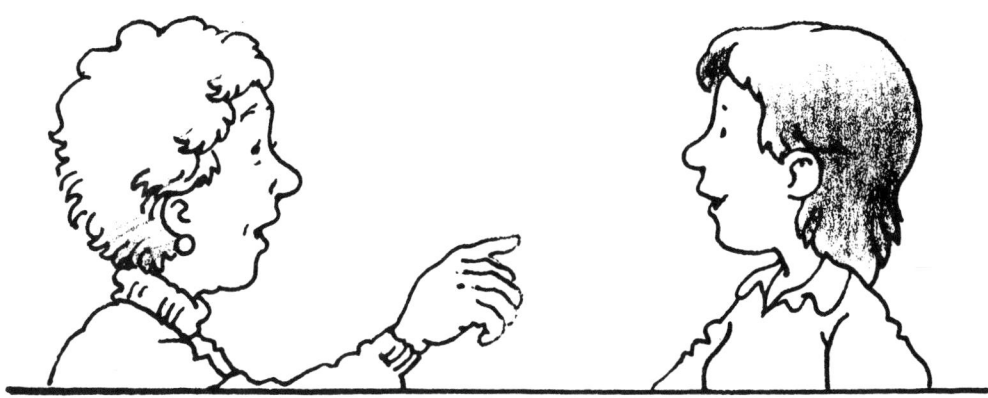

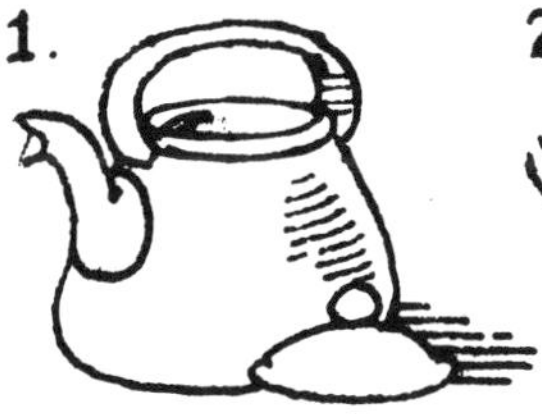

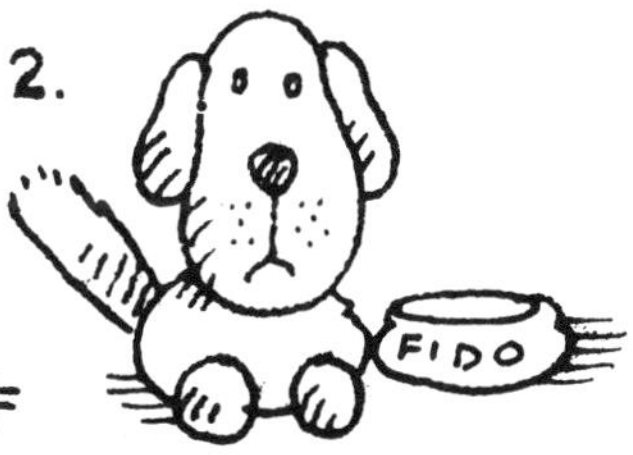

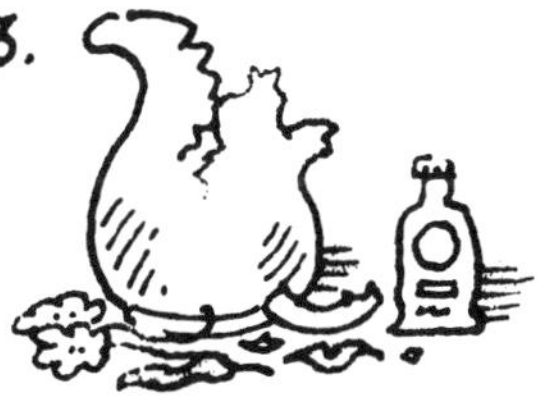

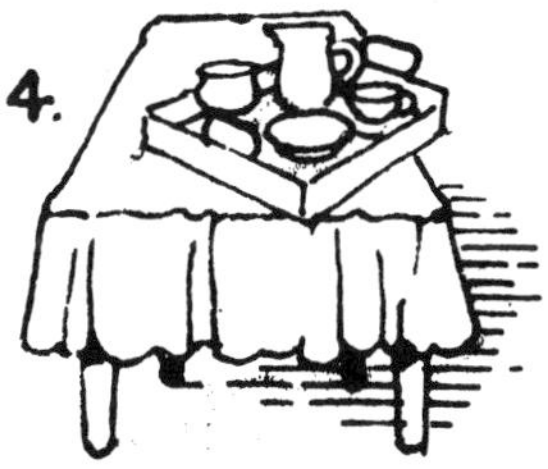

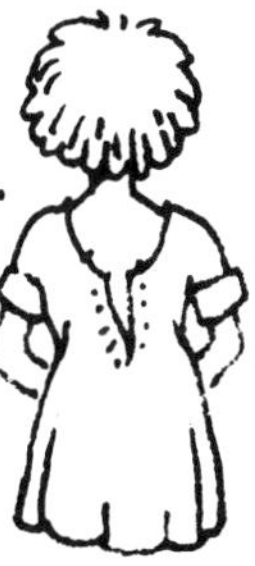

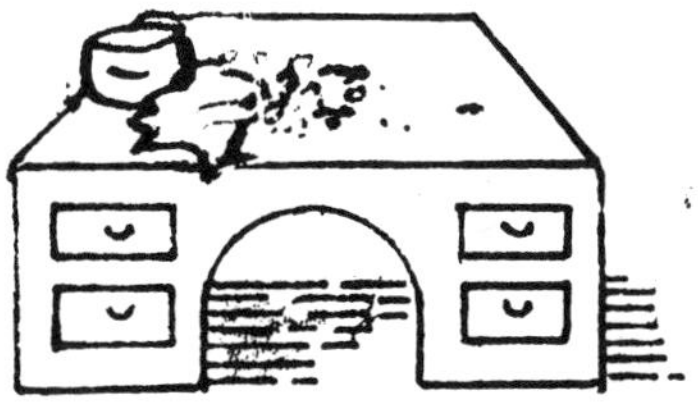

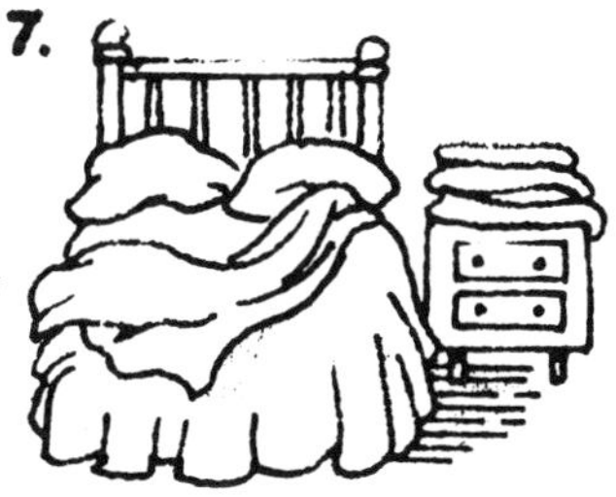

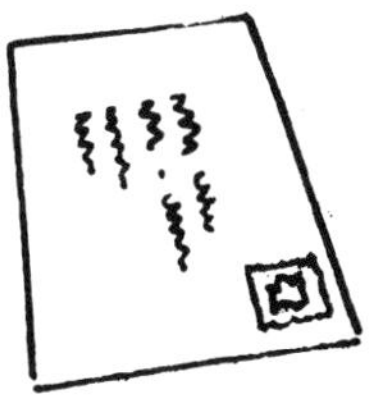

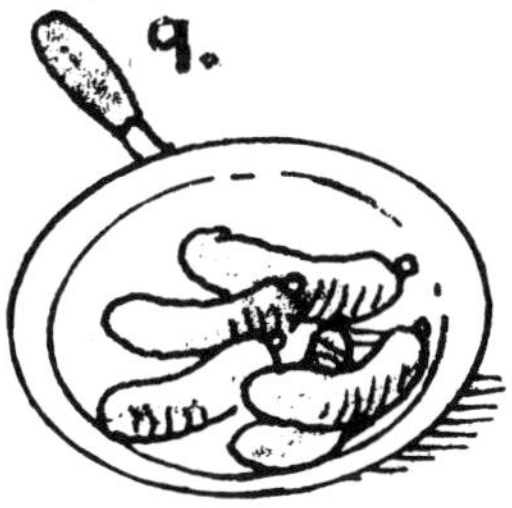

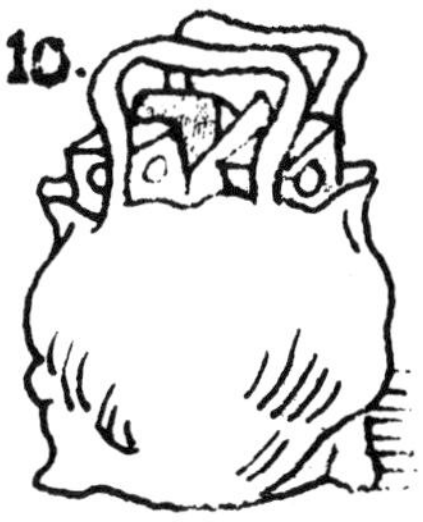

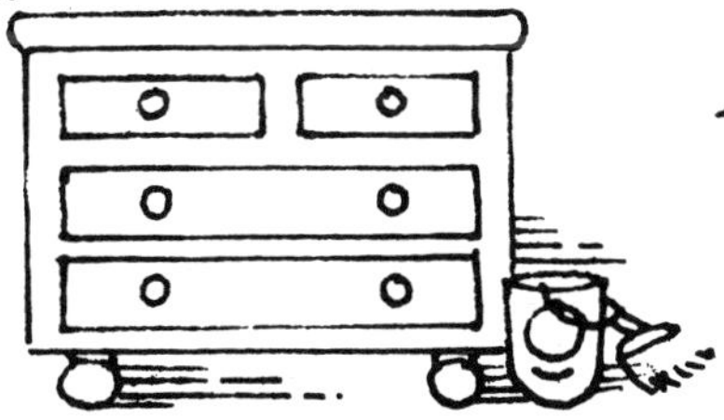

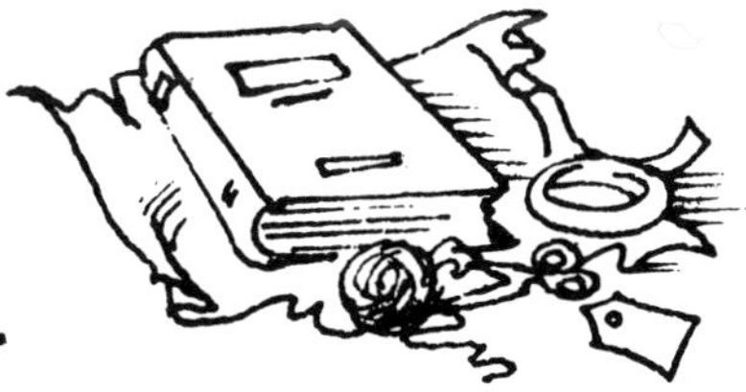

For example:
1. Please fill the kettle

1.

2.

3.

4.

5.

6.

7.

8.

9.

10.

11.

12.

13.

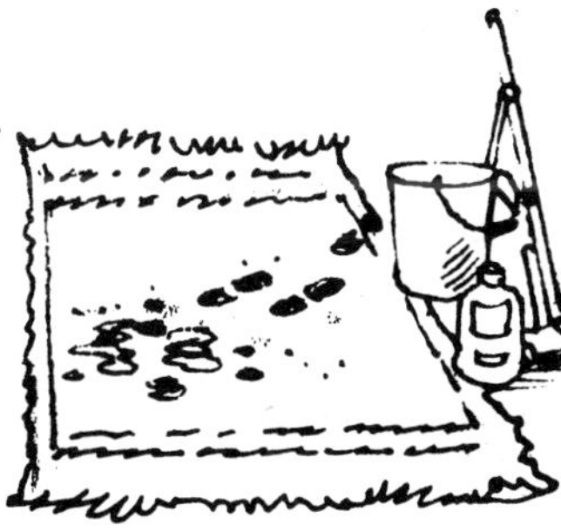

fill polish paint fasten lay cook repair
post wrap carry feed clean change

Make a Choice

Look carefully at the pictures and choose the correct answers.

For example:

1. Is it (a) a bottle of wine
   or (b) a wine bottle?   ✗

2. Is it (a) the boy's dog
   or (b) the boys' dog?

3. It is (a) a cup of coffee
   or (b) a coffee cup?

4. Is it (a) a matchbox
   or (b) a box of matches?

5. Are they (a) the farmer's son's cows
   or (b) the farmer's sons' cows?

6. Is it (a) a picture of Susan
   or (b) a picture by Susan?

7. Is it (a) a sculpture of a woman
   or (b) a sculpture by a woman?

8. Is it (a) Agatha Christie's book
   or (b) a book by Agatha Christie?

9. Is she (a) the baby's mother
   or (b) the babies' mother?

10. Is it (a) a wine glass
    or (b) a glass of wine?

PHOTOCOPIABLE

24

© Deirdre Howard-Williams and Cynthia Herd 1994
HEINEMANN ENGLISH LANGUAGE TEACHING

Shopping Centre

To buy everything on this shopping list, you must go to 13 different shops. Show the way you would go, following the numbers on the list.

1. jar of strawberry jam
2. 2 lbs of sausages
3. small brown loaf
4. 1 lb of onions
5. bandage
6. kettle
7. airmail envelopes
8. rose bush
9. 2 bars of milk chocolate
10. 2 pints of milk
11. this month's Do it Yourself magazine
12. puzzle for Sam's birthday
13. packet of fish food

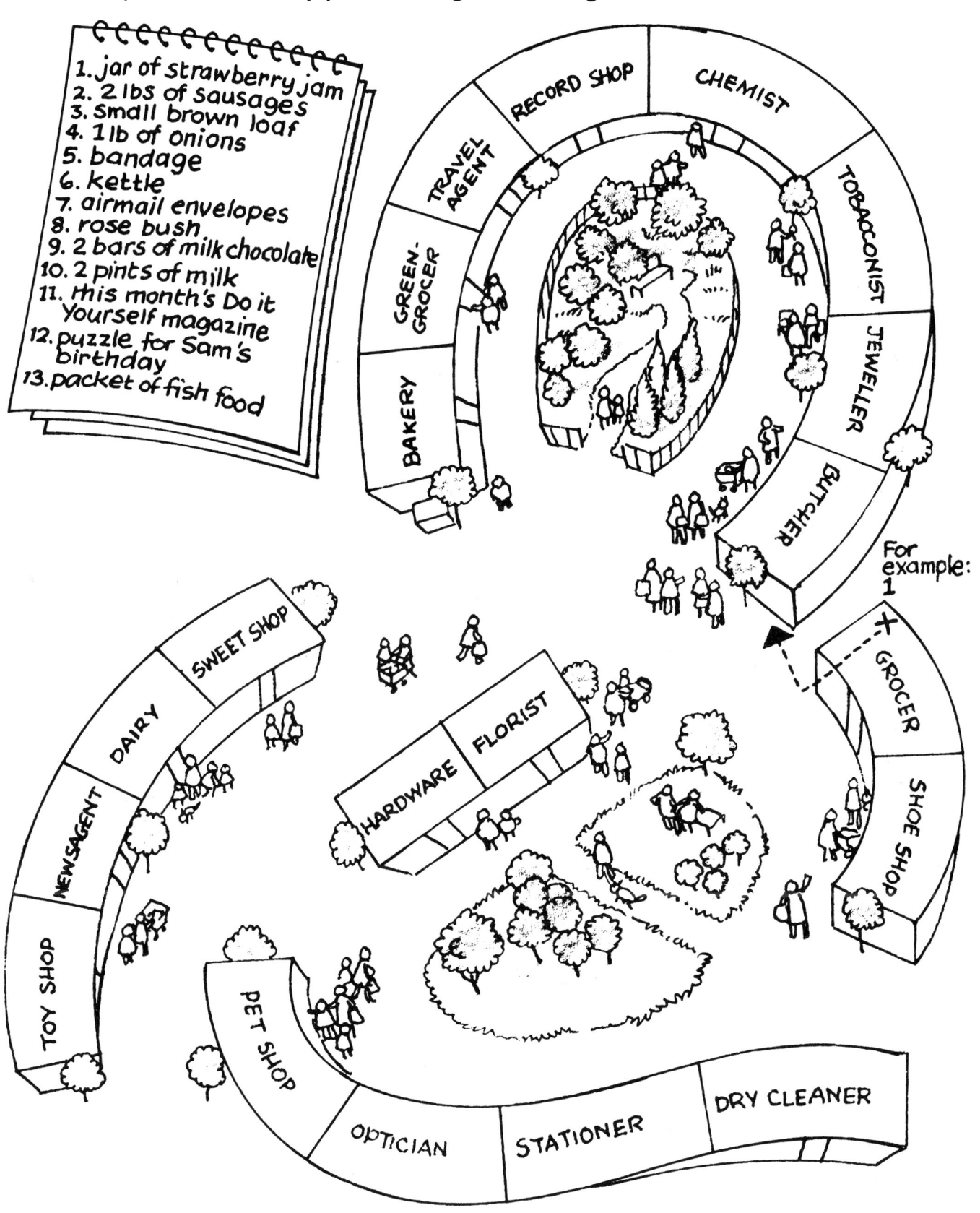

© Deirdre Howard-Williams and Cynthia Herd 1994
HEINEMANN ENGLISH LANGUAGE TEACHING

DOUBLES 1

Many words in English are made of two parts.
Put the word from list A with the correct word from list B.

For example: CENTRAL + HEATING = CENTRAL HEATING

A	B
CENTRAL	PARK
RECORD-	MINISTER
PRIME	BOX
INFORMATION	STATION
SNACK	MACHINE
DRIVING	PLAYER
BUS	ROADS
CROSS	HEATING
LETTER	DESK
CAR	LICENCE
WASHING	STOP
PETROL	BAR

© Deirdre Howard-Williams and Cynthia Herd 1994
HEINEMANN ENGLISH LANGUAGE TEACHING

Thank You

How would you say **thank you** in these situations?

For example:

visit   call   lift   help   present   party   loan   hospitality   meal   advice

Work for us!

Look at these job advertisements.
Can you fill in the missing words?

HEAD OF LANGUAGES IN PRIVATE SCHOOL
FULL _Responsibility_
HIGH _____
LONG _____
GENEROUS _____

For example:

CAR FACTORY NEEDS WORKERS
FRIENDLY _____
FREE _____
SHORT _____
SELF-SERVICE _____

WANTED SECRETARY FOR TRAVEL AGENT
PLEASANT _____
ELECTRIC _____
MODERN _____
TRAVEL _____

responsibility
canteen
holidays
office
boss
colleagues
hours
salary
typewriter
pension
transport
opportunities

© Deirdre Howard-Williams and Cynthia Herd 1994
HEINEMANN ENGLISH LANGUAGE TEACHING

Odd One OUT 2

Look at these groups of words. Find the words which do not fit.

For example:

1. BLOOD, STRAWBERRY, TOMATO, (BEER)

2. TRY ON, PUT ON, GET UP, TAKE OFF

3. GALLERY, THEATRE, CABARET, MUSEUM

4. BILL, WAITER, SERVICE CHARGE, TIP

5. COURSE, TEST, FAIL, PASS

6. CHRISTMAS, EASTER, 20TH CENTURY, NEW YEAR'S DAY

PREPOSITIONS 2

Here are 12 common expressions with **in**. Can you find them all?

For example: 1. in love

love   prison   turn   half   tears   a hurry   bed
pieces   trouble   ink   town   danger

Travel Quiz

All these words are connected with **holidays**.
Can you choose the correct explanation?

For example:

1. To **register** is
   a   to pay your bill in a hotel ☐
   b   to record your name in a hotel ☒
   c   to leave your luggage in a hotel ☐
   d   to have a meal in a hotel ☐

2. A **view** is
   a   something you taste ☐
   b   something you wear ☐
   c   something you see ☐
   d   something you hear ☐

3. A **receipt** is
   a   a kind of visa ☐
   b   a record of payment ☐
   c   an insurance document ☐
   d   a single ticket ☐

4. A **hotel guest** is
   a   a person who works in a hotel ☐
   b   a person who is waiting to get a room ☐
   c   a person who is staying at the hotel ☐
   d   a person who recommends hotels ☐

5. A **caravan** is
   a   used to sit on ☐
   b   used to lie on ☐
   c   used to live in ☐
   d   used to sail with ☐

6. A **message** is
   a   a snack ☐
   b   a friend ☐
   c   a piece of news ☐
   d   a parcel ☐

7. A **flight** is
   a   a trip by air ☐
   b   a trip by sea ☐
   c   a trip by train ☐
   d   a trip by car ☐

8. **Abroad** is
   a   outside your own country ☐
   b   in your country ☐
   c   when you are on holiday ☐
   d   in Europe ☐

9. A **youth hostel** is
   a   a kind of reduction for young people ☐
   b   a kind of hotel ☐
   c   a kind of exhibition ☐
   d   a kind of children's room ☐

10. A **fare** is
    a   an amusement park ☐
    b   a place to put your luggage ☐
    c   an extra charge on a bill ☐
    d   the price of a journey ☐

11. **Welcome** is
    a   a greeting ☐
    b   a food ☐
    c   a class of hotel ☐
    d   a warning ☐

12. A **frontier** is
    a   a foreign currency ☐
    b   a foreign country ☐
    c   between two countries ☐
    d   an immigration form ☐

© Deirdre Howard-Williams and Cynthia Herd 1994
HEINEMANN ENGLISH LANGUAGE TEACHING

WHERE DOES IT GO?

Identify the objects in A and B. Each object from A can go into one of the objects in B. Can you put them together?

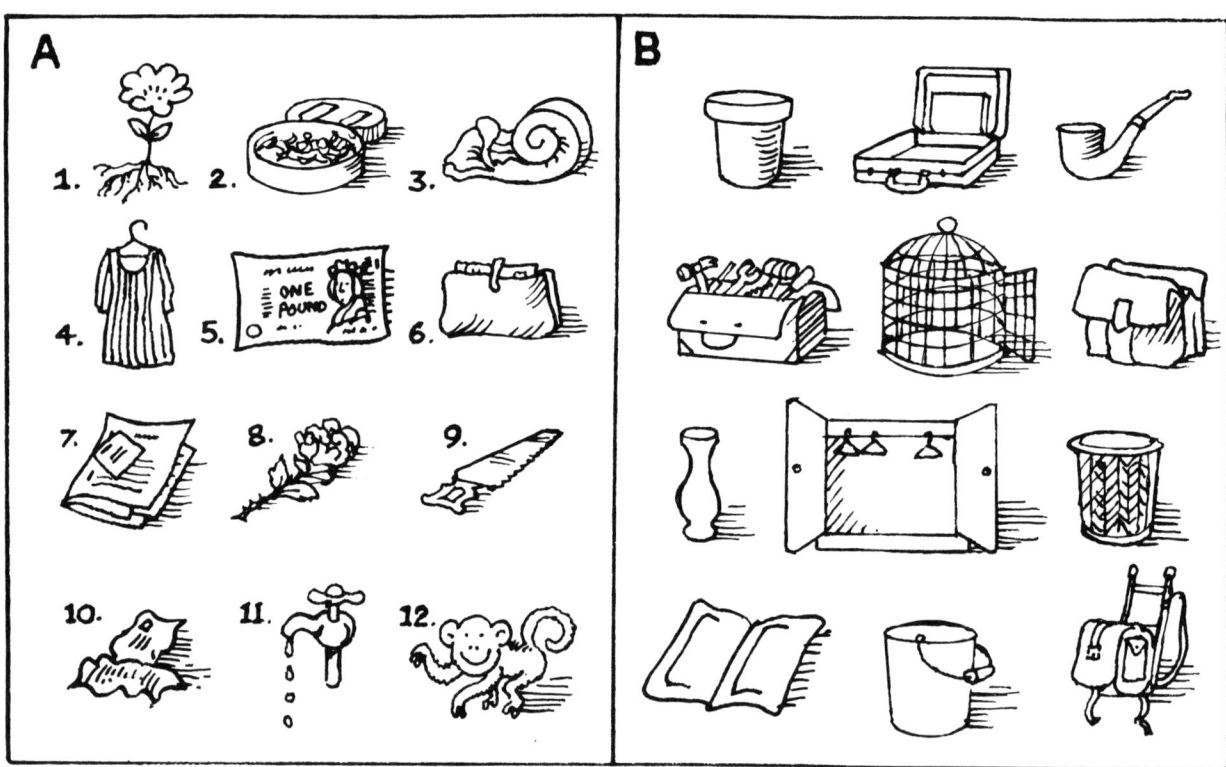

plant   document   rubbish
evening dress   rose   water
sleeping bag   monkey   saw
pound note   tobacco   purse

flower pot   wallet   cage
rucksack   wastepaper basket
vase   pipe   wardrobe   tool box
handbag   briefcase   bucket

For example:

1. A plant goes in a flower pot
2. Tobacco
3.
4.
5.
6.
7.
8.
9.
10.
11.
12.

32

© Deirdre Howard-Williams and Cynthia Herd 1994
HEINEMANN ENGLISH LANGUAGE TEACHING

CROSSWORD 2

All the answers are connected with **entertainment**.

© Deirdre Howard-Williams and Cynthia Herd 1994
HEINEMANN ENGLISH LANGUAGE TEACHING

Prefixes & Suffixes

MINI- NON- SELF-

UN- RE-

-ABLE -ER -Y

-ESE -FUL -ESS -LESS

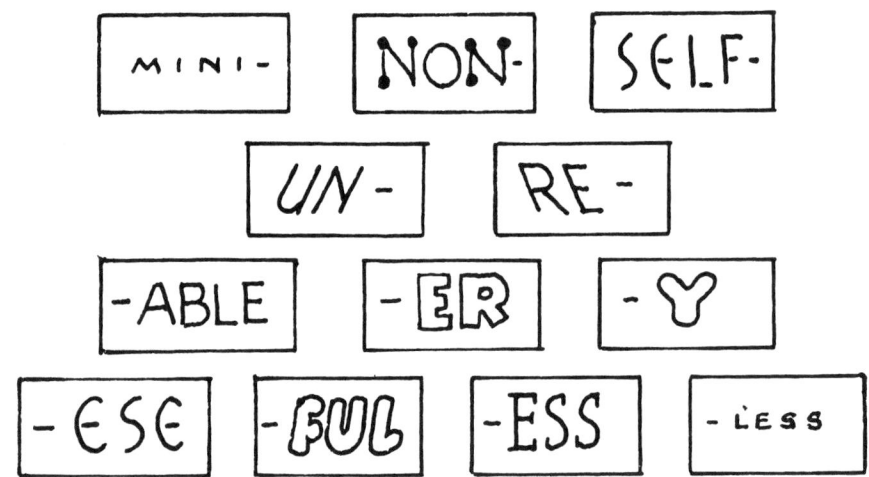

Can you put them in the correct place?

For example: useless

1. USE

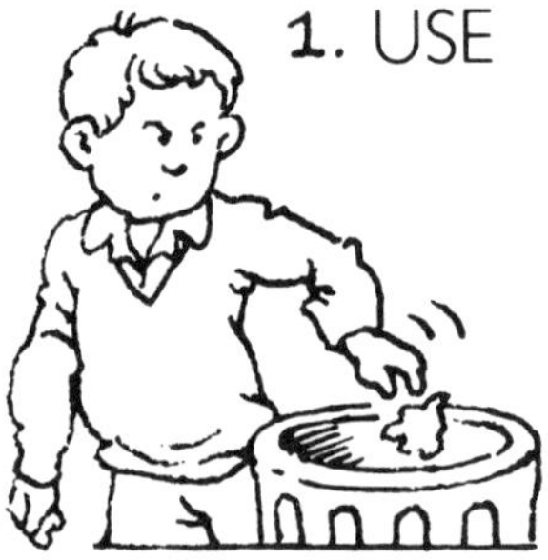

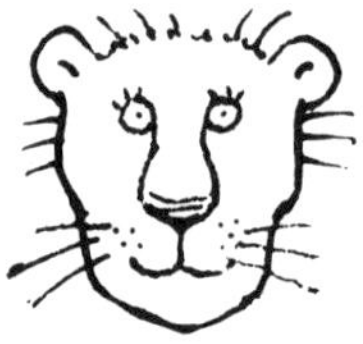

2. LION

3. SERVICE

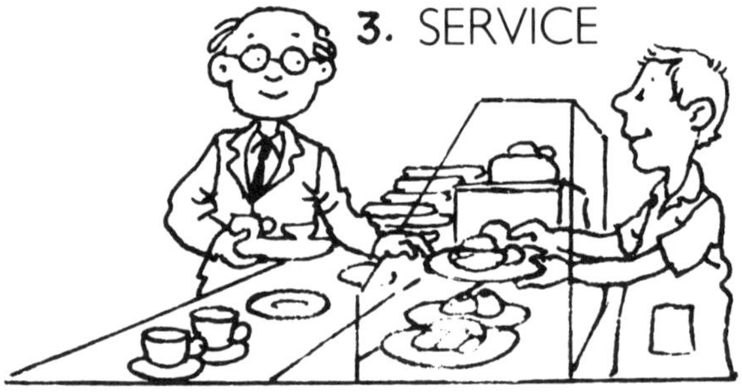

4. SPOON

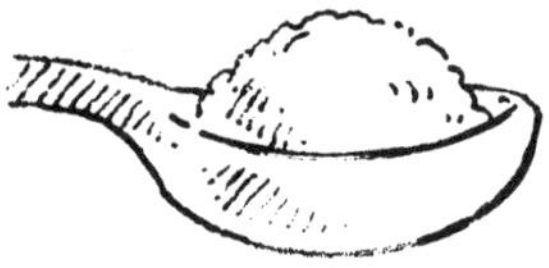

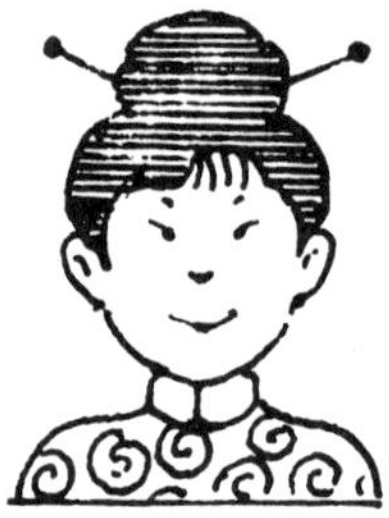

5. JAPAN

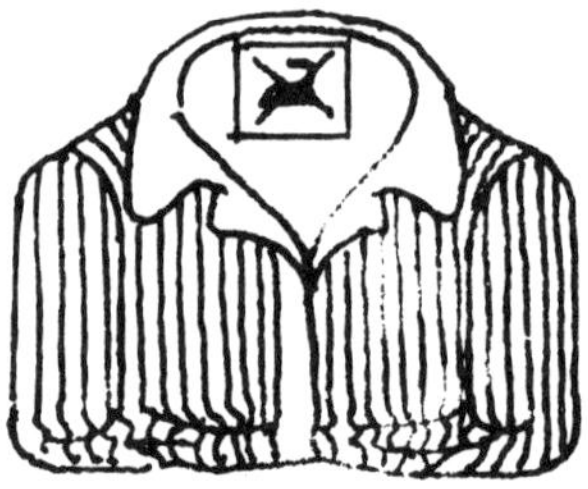

6. IRON

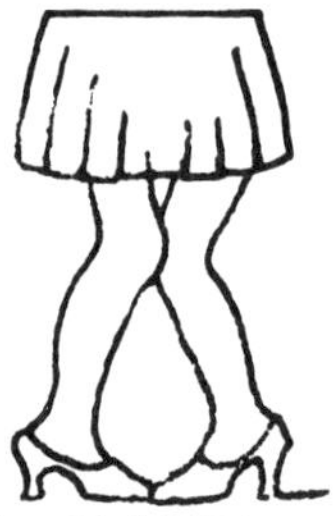

7. SKIRT

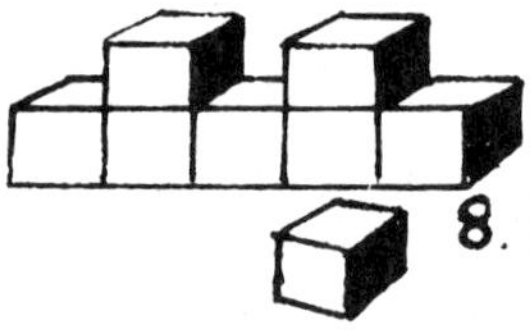

8. BUILD

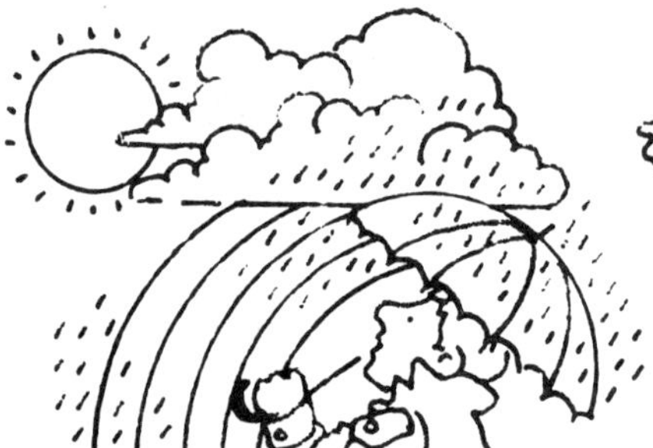

9. CHANGE

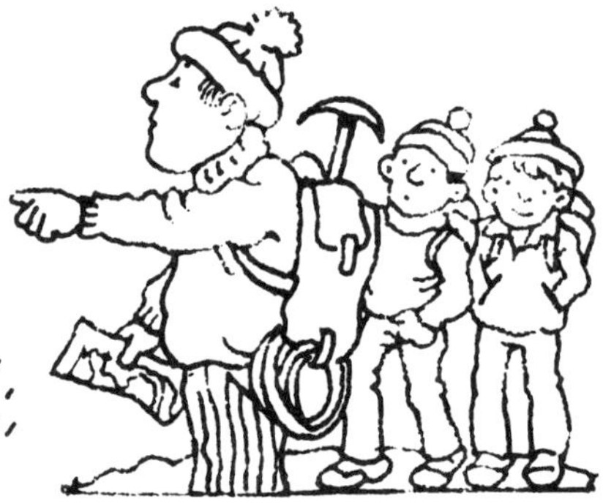

10. LEAD

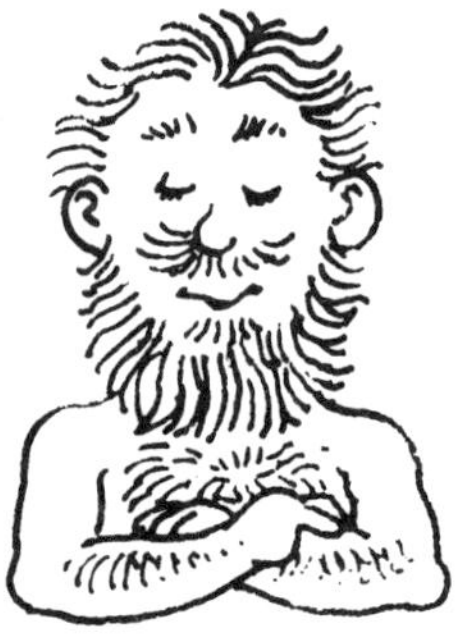

11. HAIR

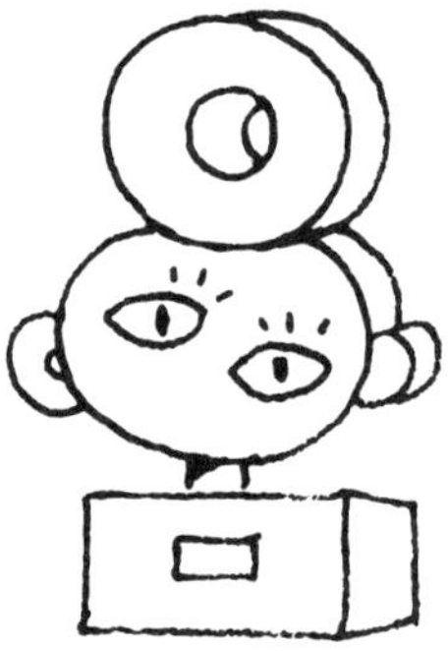

12. USUAL

IN THE PRESS

All these items are from pages of a newspaper. Can you fill in the Contents List?

page 2
WHERE GRADUATES GO

	Permanent UK work %	Further study %
Art & Design	41.5	9.0
Biological Sciences	34.6	27.5
Business Management	75.8	3.5
Chemistry	37.6	34.2

page 14

Sagittarius

page 4
OPERA AND BALLET

ROYAL OPERA HOUSE COVENT GARDEN. Resv.: 01-240 1066/1911 Access, Visa, Diners Club. S. Standby info. 01-836 6903. 65 amphi seats available from 10 am on the day. Tickets Opera £2.00-£34.00 Ballet £1.00-£20.00.

page 9
Sir, Today I saw my bank manager with a shovel in his hands. He was outside the bank, alone, chipping frozen snow from the pavement.
  A sign of the times?
Yours truly,

page 7
BBC 1 Wales: 8.30-9.00am Rugby Union: Try, try again. 5.15-5.20pm Sports News Wales. 12.30-12.35am News. Scotland: 12.15-5.05pm Grandstand. Including Rugby Union

page 4
CLARE. On February 21st at King's College Hospital to Jane (nee Hogan) And Anthony, a son Sebastian, a brother for Rachel, Simon, Eleanor, Peter, Sophie and Justine.

page 13
TENNIS
ROSENHEIM, West Germany: Winter circuit tournament, quarter-finals: H-D Beutel (WG) bt A Zveren (USSR), 6-3, 6-7, 7-5; S Birner (Cz) bt C Zipf (WG), 6-2, 6-3; F Segarceanu (Rom) bt W Popp (WG), 6-2, 3-6, 6-3; P Carlsson (Swe) bt U Fischer (WG), 6-3, 7-6.

page 10
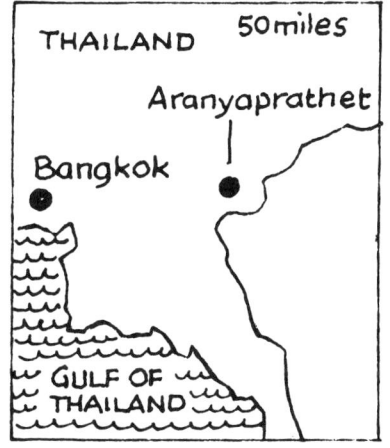

page 12
LONDON COMMODITY PRICES
Rubber in £'s per tonne;
Coffee, cocoa, sugar
in pounds per metric ton;
Gas-oil in US $
per metric tonne.
G W Joynson and Co report

COCOA
Mar	2118-15
May	2135-34
Jly	2119-16
Sep	2104-03

page 6
WINTER SPORTS
SKI WHIZZ
NO 1 FOR CHALET FUN!
Superb resorts   Inclusive prices!
March 16 £209   March 30 £229
March 23 £259   April 6 £219
         April 13 £164
FILL A CHALET — YOU GO FREE!

Contents
	Page
For example: Careers Information	2
	4
	4
	5
	6
	7
	9
	10
	12
	12
	13
	14

page 5
Solution of Puzzle No 16,657

page 12

PINE SALE ENDS SUNDAY — THE LARGEST STOCK OF FINEST QUALITY SOLID PINE FURNITURE AT THE VERY KEENEST PRICES IN YOUR AREA. Nationwide deliveries. Write or phone for lists. Goldpine Furniture.

Careers Information   Travel & Holidays   Readers' Letters   Foreign News
Horoscopes   Births, Marriages & Deaths   Entertainments Guide
Advertisements   TV & Radio   Sport   Crossword   Business

BOOKS

Here are 12 students working in the college library.
Look carefully at the titles of the books they are reading.
What subjects are the students studying?

For example: 1. He is studying poetry

poetry   jazz appreciation   psychology   antiques   first aid
the modern novel   keep fit   translation   dressmaking
wine-making   banking   computer science.

The Word Snake

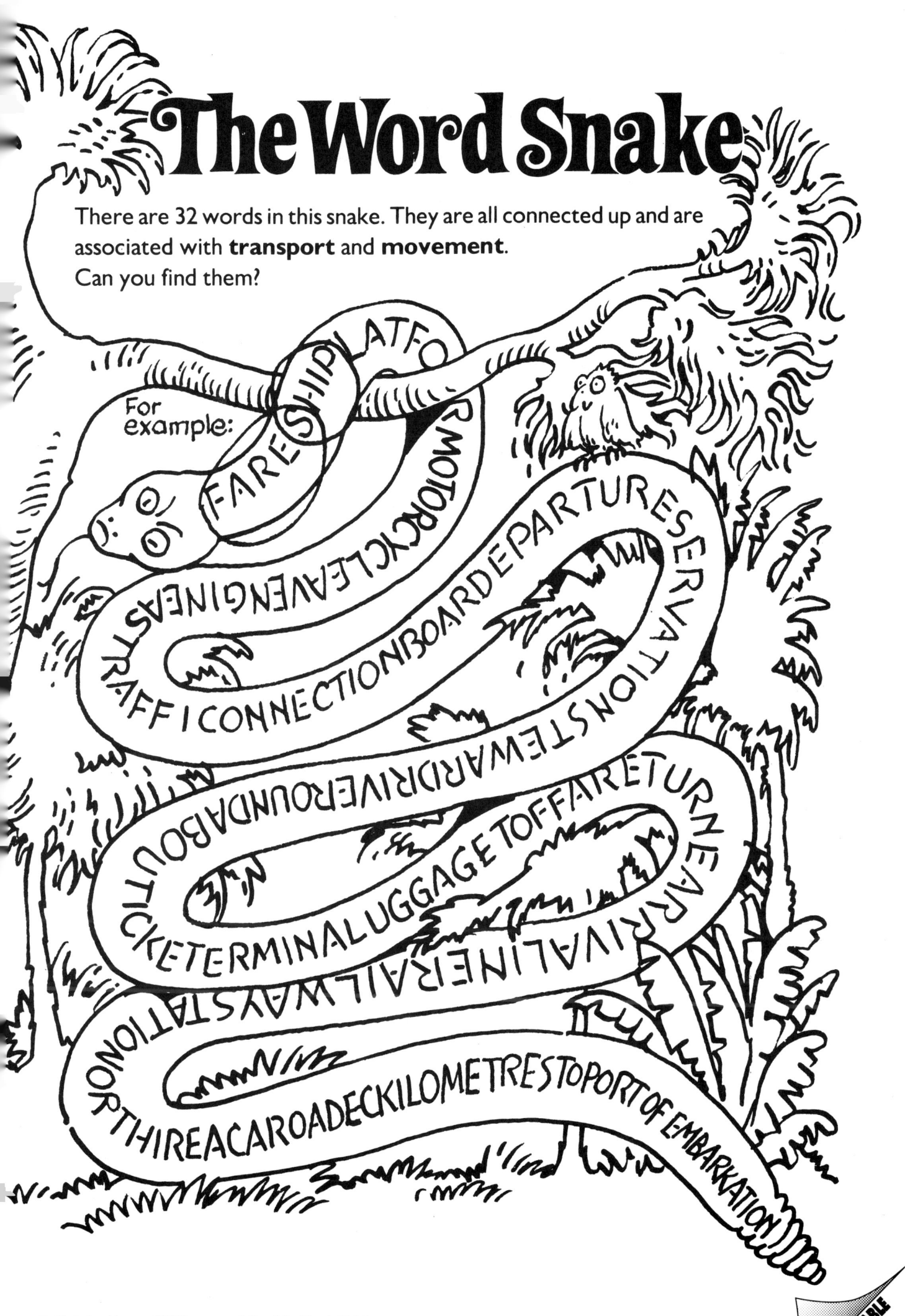

There are 32 words in this snake. They are all connected up and are associated with **transport** and **movement**. Can you find them?

For example: FARE–SHIP–PLATFORM...

FARESHIPLATFORMOTORCYCLEAVENGINESTRAFFICONNECTIONBOARDEPARTURESERVATIONSTEWARDRIVEROUNDABOUTICKETERMINALUGGAGETOFFARETURNEARRIVALRAILWAYSTATIONORTHIREACAROADECKILOMETRESTOPORTOFEMBARKATION

© Deirdre Howard-Williams and Cynthia Herd 1994
HEINEMANN ENGLISH LANGUAGE TEACHING

PHOTOCOPIABLE

Time Off

These 6 people have different plans for their time off. What things do they need?

For example:

1. parasol
2.
3.
4.
5.
6.

1. I'M GOING TO THE BEACH.
2. I'M GOING TO MAKE SOME CURTAINS.
3. I'M GOING FISHING.
4. I'M GOING TO REDECORATE THE BATHROOM.
5. I'M GOING WALKING IN THE MOUNTAINS
6. I'M GOING TO LOOK AFTER MY BABY NIECE FOR THE WEEKEND.

parasol swimsuit rod needle nappies line plaster
climbing boots cot deck-chair compass hook thread stick
material push-chair net wallpaper rope suntan lotion
tape measure tiles paste talcum powder

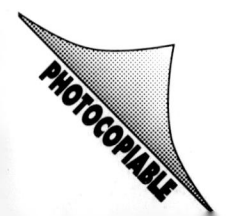

The word snail

There are 30 words in this word snail. They are all connected up and describe what you might see in the English countryside. Can you find them?

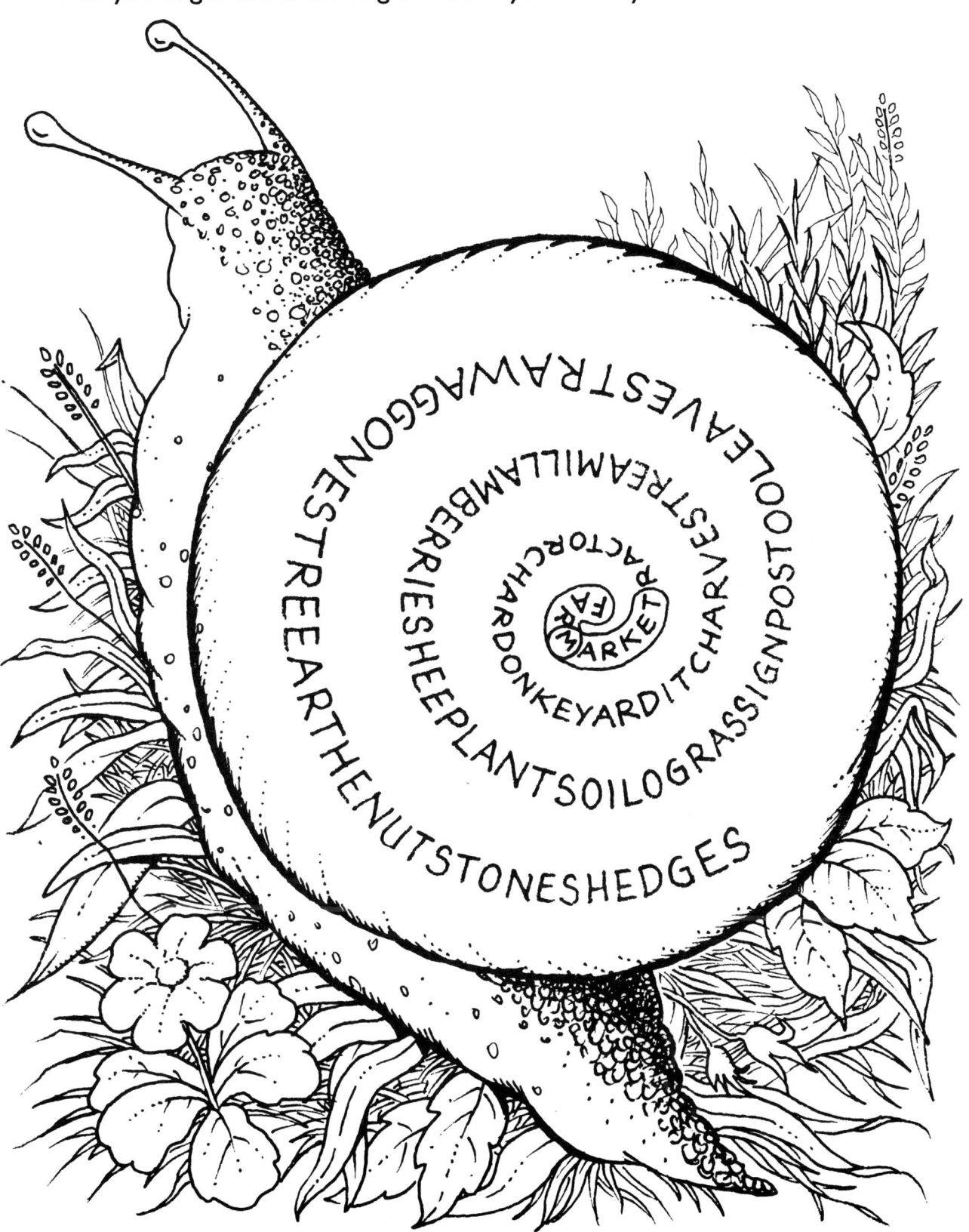

Spiral text (from outside in): TREEEARTHENUTSTONESHEDGESNOGGAWARTSEVAELOOTSOPNGISSARGOLIOSTNALPPEEHSREBMALLIMAERTSHCTIDRAYEKNODRAHCROTCAFTEKRAM

Unwound: TREE · EARTH · NUTS · STONES · HEDGES · WAGGON · STREAM ... MARKET (reading inward)

© Deirdre Howard-Williams and Cynthia Herd 1994
HEINEMANN ENGLISH LANGUAGE TEACHING

PHOTOCOPIABLE

Words easily confused

These pairs of words are often confused.
Look at the picture and choose the correct word.

For example:

1. prize/(price)
2. channel/canal
3. hotel/hostel
4. professor/teacher
5. audience/spectators
6. doctor/surgeon
7. assistant/attendant
8. fault/mistake
9. bank/shore
10. fees/salary
11. journey/voyage
12. bath/bathe
13. newspaper/magazine
14. hedge/fence
15. duty/tax
16. housework/homework

DOUBLES 2

Look at each picture. Then put one word from column A with another word from column B to form a compound which describes the picture. It may be one word, 2 words, or hyphenated.

For example: 1. Boarding pass.

A	B
BOARDING	RING
THUNDER	HANDED
EVENING	SHADE
YOUTH	BULLETIN
SECONDARY	STORM
LEFT-	MADE
OPENING	HAND
FALSE	PASS
NEWS	CLASS
HOME-	HOURS
TIME	HOSTEL
SECOND-	CHARGE
SERVICE	SCHOOL
EAR	TEETH
LAMP	TABLE

© Deirdre Howard-Williams and Cynthia Herd 1994
HEINEMANN ENGLISH LANGUAGE TEACHING

Words beginning with CAR-

Here are 12 words which begin with CAR-. The pictures and the number of letters will help you to complete the words.

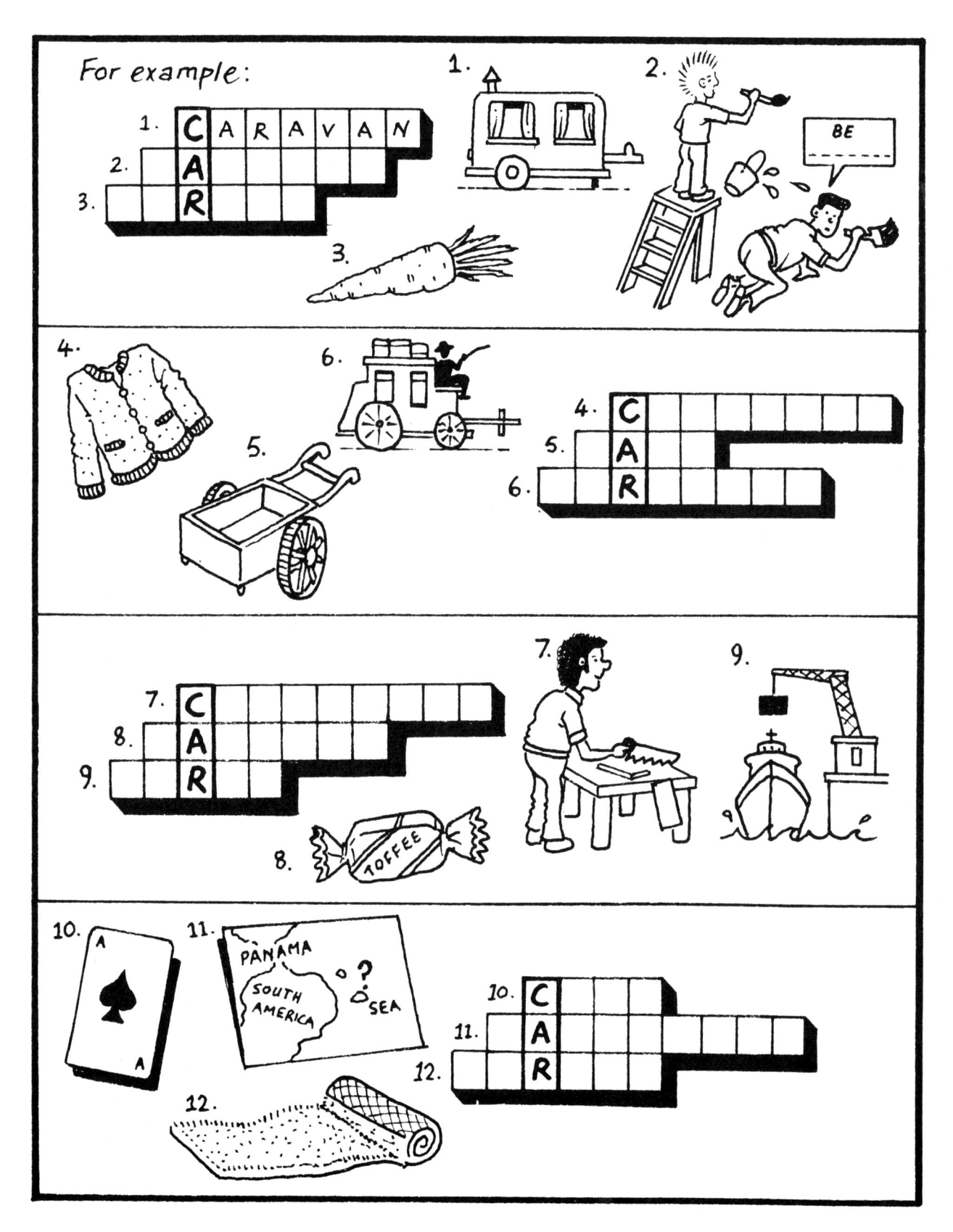

Odd One OUT 3

Here are 8 groups of adjectives.
Which word is the odd one out in each group?

For example:

1. speedy
   (slow)
   swift
   rapid

2. huge
   enormous
   immense
   tiny

3. pretty
   graceful
   handsome
   ugly

4. reduced
   costly
   unreasonable
   dear

5. glad
   sad
   merry
   cheerful

6. rusty
   spotless
   stained
   dusty

7. scared
   frightened
   cowardly
   bold

8. sickly
   healthy
   sound
   fit

Make and do

Do you know how to use MAKE and DO correctly?
With the words below to help you, decide whether to use MAKE or DO to describe the pictures.
DO your best and try not to MAKE a mistake.

For example: 1. Make progress.

progress   housework   joke   choice   washing-up   speech   shopping
trouble   friends   cake   film   homework   effort   business   faces
gardening

Words and meanings

Many words in English have more than one meaning.
Look at the 2 different meanings and try to find the word which describes them both.

For example:

1. with pages/to reserve — B O O K
2. sides of a river/safe for money
3. page of a book/grows on a tree
4. teach a person/goes on rails
5. a sound in music/piece of paper money
6. walk with it/fix with glue
7. green area/place and leave a car
8. circle or strip of material/plays music
9. to go down/used to wash up in
10. to hit lightly/where water comes from
11. flat surface/takes off and lands
12. alter/money
13. fight with gloves/square container
14. factory/in the ground
15. a point at school/a sign
16. to note and remember/musical disc
17. a pillar/send a letter
18. noted with eyes/cuts trees
19. run to win/a whole nation
20. to give/part of body
21. traffic block/fruit and sugar

THE WASTEPAPER BASKET

For example: 1 A label

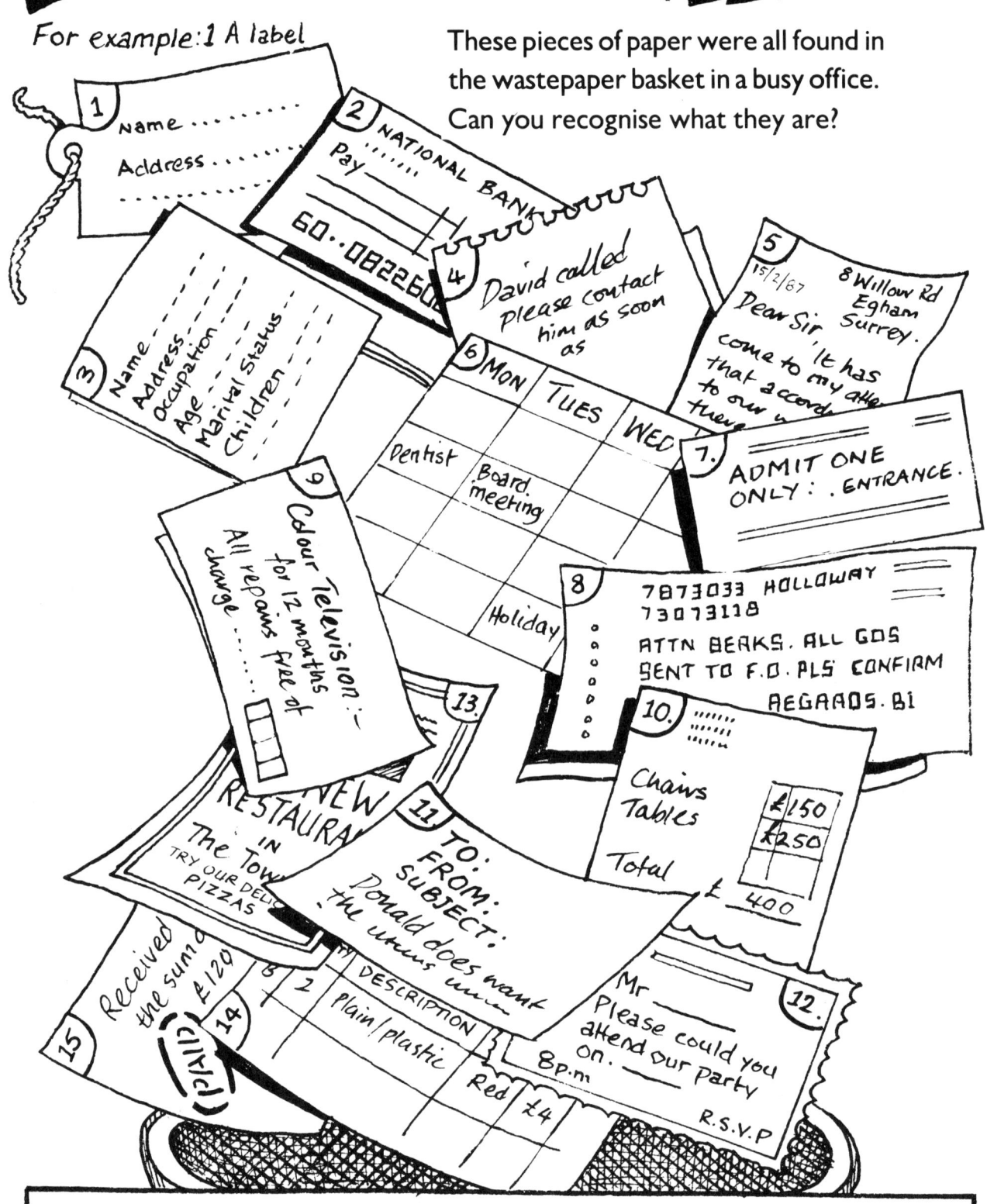

These pieces of paper were all found in the wastepaper basket in a busy office. Can you recognise what they are?

order form   bill   timetable   guarantee   letter   telex   label   ticket
cheque   application form   invitation   telephone message   receipt
memo   advertisement

The Name Game

Parts of 20 names are shown in the picture clues. Fill in the names beside the correct pictures. The first 12 are boys' names.

For example:

1. STEPHEN

Robert Irene Philip Mary Anthony Ruth Stephen Matthew
Janice Thomas Pamela Janet Simon Harold James Keith Wendy
Sandra Vera Peter Yvonne Richard Caroline Ernest Jim
Joan Rosemary Hugh Rachel Victor Patrick Alison Eric Martin

© Deirdre Howard-Williams and Cynthia Herd 1994
HEINEMANN ENGLISH LANGUAGE TEACHING

CROSS IT OUT

Read the 15 clues and cross out the 2 correct answers each time.
Finally you will be left with just 1 word.

For example: 1.

violin ~~windscreen~~ ~~brake~~
ceiling slides
ankle pink Jupiter fees
ring accountant honey
Panama Communism guitar
nuts scarf shorts
prints
rent Suez
purple Socialism doorway
Catholicism coin
chin Judaism architect puzzle Mars

Clues

1. 2 parts of a car
2. 2 colours
3. 2 jobs
4. 2 religions
5. 2 things that are round
6. 2 planets
7. 2 canals
8. 2 things you pay
9. 2 parts of the body
10. 2 kinds of photograph
11. 2 political beliefs
12. 2 things you eat
13. 2 musical instruments
14. 2 things you can wear
15. 2 parts of a room

So ... which word is left?

What's on the menu?

Use all the words given below to complete this menu.

Ernie's Restaurant
MENU

STARTERS

For example:
- Prawn Cocktail

FISH

MEAT

VEGETABLES

DESSERTS

DRINKS

---

prawn   of the day   minerals   pie   plain   fresh   Dover   chilled   steak
avocado   wine   brussel   creamed   melon   meringue pie
and Yorkshire pudding   boiled rice   fruit   with parsley sauce   fruit salad
chocolate   soup   new   cocktail   Madras   cauliflower   real   and kidney pie
red   house   chicken   curry   sprouts   English ale   mousse   juices
roast beef   cheesecake   pear   by the glass   baked ham   fried plaice
grilled   potatoes   mackerel   and pineapple   seafood   with cream
lemon   sole

Connections

Can you find 2 letters which will finish the first word and start the second word?

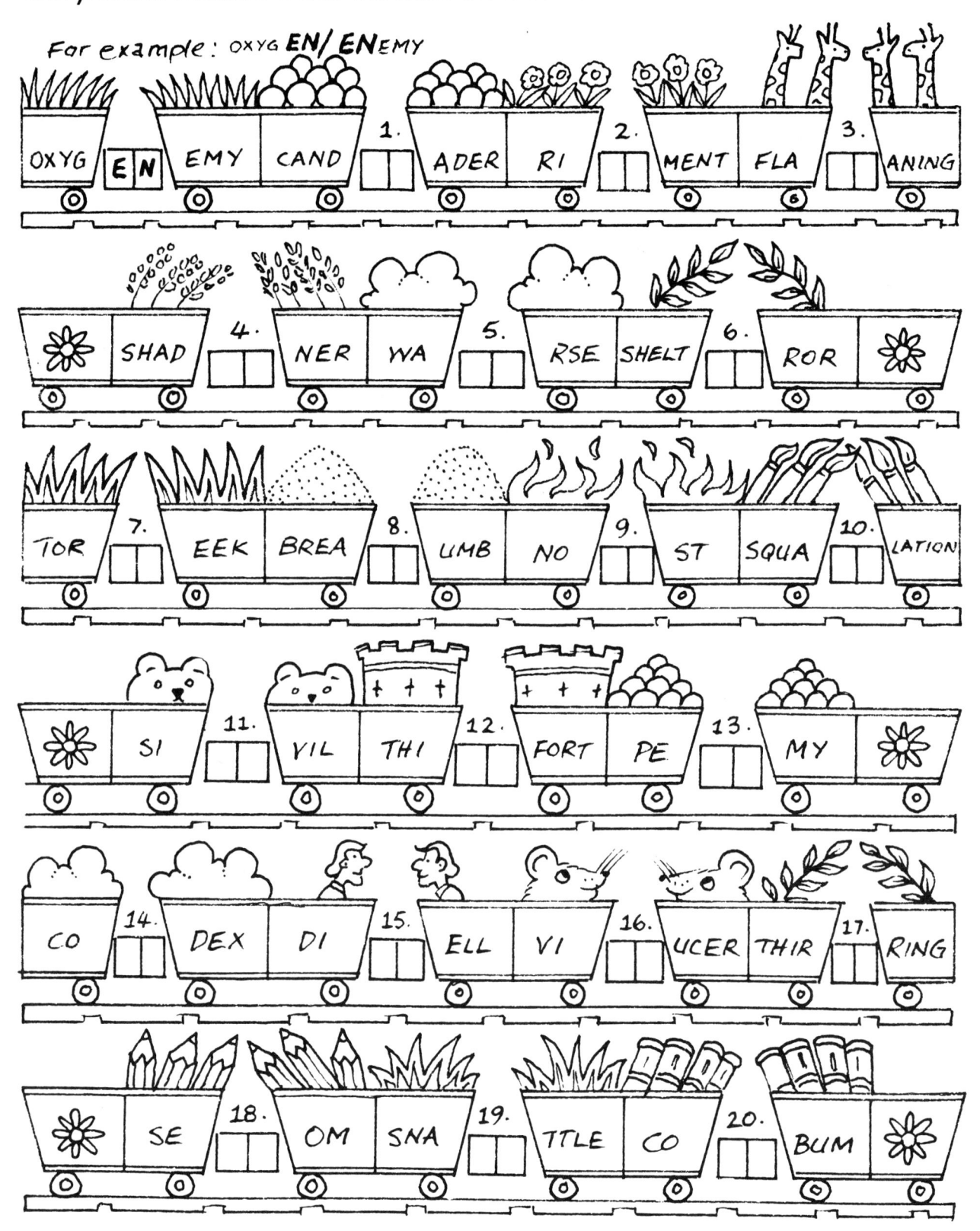

For example: OXYG **EN**/**EN**emy

1. OXYG [EN] EMY CAND [__] ADER RI [2.] MENT FLA [3.] ANING
2. SHAD [4.] NER WA [5.] RSE SHELT [6.] ROR
3. TOR [7.] EEK BREA [8.] UMB NO [9.] ST SQUA [10.] LATION
4. SI [11.] VIL THI [12.] FORT PE [13.] MY
5. CO [14.] DEX DI [15.] ELL VI [16.] UCER THIR [17.] RING
6. SE [18.] OM SNA [19.] TTLE CO [20.] BUM

© Deirdre Howard-Williams and Cynthia Herd 1994
HEINEMANN ENGLISH LANGUAGE TEACHING

PHOTOCOPIABLE

The Family Tree

Look at Steve's family tree and the list of his relations.
Write the names of Steve's relations.

For example: 1. Sidney is Steve's grandfather.

1. SIDNEY
2. MAY
3. JOHN
4. ALICE
5. RAY
6. VERA
7. ALAN (Married 1957) Ⓑ
8. RUTH
9. ROGER (Died 1955) Ⓐ
10. CHRISTOPHER
11. DORIS
12. NANCY
13. ANN
14. DAVE
15. MARY (Divorced 1972) Ⓐ
16. PAM (Married 1973) Ⓑ
17. ADAM
18. IRENE
19. JUNE
20. ERIC
21. JOY
22. WENDY
23. TRACY

aunt   first wife   mother-in-law   grandmother   daughter
daughter-in-law   mother   uncle   grandfather   nephew   father-in-law
cousin   sister-in-law   step-father   second wife   step-daughter   niece
brother   granddaughter   son   father

© Deirdre Howard-Williams and Cynthia Herd 1994
HEINEMANN ENGLISH LANGUAGE TEACHING

Words ending in -TION

A lot of words in English end in -TION. Here are 12 of them. The pictures and the number of letters will help you to complete the words.

THE S CONNECTION

There are some nouns which exist only in the plural form. Look at this picture and see how many plural-form nouns you can find.
(Clue: There are more than 10 but less than 20).

For example: Customs.

Collectives

Here are 16 collective nouns for describing groups of people or things. They are all placed against the wrong pictures. Match each word with the correct picture.

For example: 1. Staff

1	jury
2	fleet
3	queue
4	club
5	collection
6	staff
7	crew
8	committee
9	union
10	flock
11	team
12	bunch
13	audience
14	crowd
15	class
16	orchestra

© Deirdre Howard-Williams and Cynthia Herd 1994
HEINEMANN ENGLISH LANGUAGE TEACHING

PHOTOCOPIABLE

COMPLAINTS

Complain about these things you have bought. Something is wrong. Look at the pictures and use the correct words to describe them.

For example: 1. It's melted.

melted   bad   blunt   loose   dusty   slow   bent   stretched
cracked   leaking   overripe   dirty   scratched   torn   broken

© Deirdre Howard-Williams and Cynthia Herd 1994
HEINEMANN ENGLISH LANGUAGE TEACHING

LANGUAGE FUNCTIONS

Look at this picture of men busy building a factory, and note what they are saying and doing.

- H. They're my favourite team.
- O. I wi...
- B. Why don't you have a rest?
- I. Yes they play well, but this team is better.
- A. You should get a smaller one.
- C. I'm not sure you'll do it
- F. Wow, Look at that!
- J. You can go home now.
- G. Well done! Tha... very clever.
- D. Would you like one?
- K. Oh ... so...
- E. Oh, thank you very much.

PHOTOCOPIABLE

© Deirdre Howard-Williams and Cynthia Herd 1994
HEINEMANN ENGLISH LANGUAGE TEACHING

For example: 1F

Find someone expressing:
1. surprise F
2. doubt
3. certainty
4. likes
5. preferences
6. gratitude
7. sympathy

Find someone making:
8. an apology
9. a complaint
10. a request
11. an offer
12. a suggestion
13. a criticism

Find someone giving:
14. a warning
15. advice
16. an explanation
17. an order
18. permission
19. an opinion
20. a compliment

N. Yes, I'm sure there's enough room.

P. Could I have a bucket please?

S. Look out!

...fit.

...has to be ...is for roof.

Mend this immediately!

M. You poor man! How awful!

...an't you be ...ore careful!

T. Your work isn't good enough.

© Deirdre Howard-Williams and Cynthia Herd 1994
HEINEMANN ENGLISH LANGUAGE TEACHING

PROVERBS

Here are 8 well-known English proverbs. Can you write them out in full?

For example: 1. A stitch in time saves nine.

1. A 🪡 in 🕐 saves 9.

2. A 🐦 in the ✋ is worth 2 in the 🌳.

3. An 🧑's 🏠 is his 🏰.

4. Many ✋✋✋ make 💡 work.

5. ½ a 🍞 is better than ◯.

6. 1 🧑's 🍖 is another 🧑's ☠️.

7. U can lead a 🐴 2 💧 but U can't make him 🥤.

8. 👥 in 🍷 🏠 should not throw 🪨.

DOUBLES 3

Can you make another 12 compounds? Look at each picture. Then put one word from column A with another word from column B to form a compound which describes the picture. It may be one word, 2 words or hyphenated.

For example: 1. Charter flight

A	B
CHARTER	NAILS
DISH	SITTER
BOARDING	PASS
WATER	FLIGHT
OFFICE	PAPER
OPERA	HOUSE
BY	WASHER
TOE	PROOF
SIGHT	SEEING
NOTE	SCHOOL
NATIVE	LANGUAGE
BABY-	WORKER

12. "I'M ENGLISH"

© Deirdre Howard-Williams and Cynthia Herd 1994
HEINEMANN ENGLISH LANGUAGE TEACHING

The Weather Forecast

Can you find 15 words connected with WEATHER in this word square? The words are horizontal ⌒, vertical ◯, or diagonal ⌒.

For example:

L	L	K	J	M	I	G	S	H	S
F	I	C	Y	F	I	E	H	S	U
R	R	G	A	L	E	L	A	H	N
O	A	E	H	E	A	T	D	O	S
S	V	Z	E	T	Y	X	E	W	H
T	V	E	U	Z	N	W	B	E	I
D	R	T	R	S	E	I	C	R	N
W	A	R	M	C	J	E	N	I	E
Q	N	M	L	K	A	E	F	G	C
P	O	M	P	M	I	S	T	B	Z
S	T	O	R	M	H	G	T	A	D

© Deirdre Howard-Williams and Cynthia Herd 1994
HEINEMANN ENGLISH LANGUAGE TEACHING

PHOTOCOPIABLE

PURCHASES

Look at these 4 articles and fill in the labels describing them.

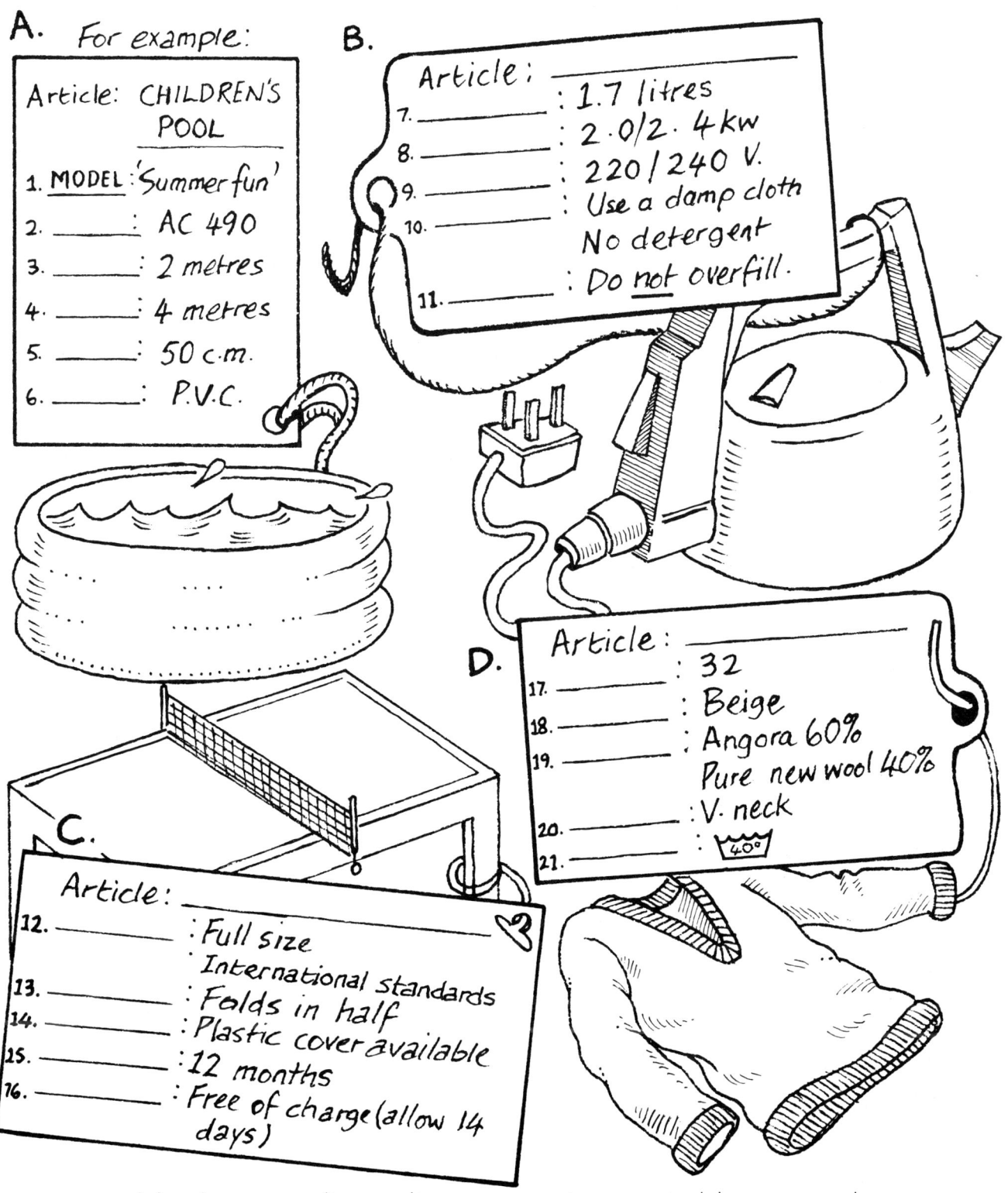

A. For example:

Article: CHILDREN'S POOL

1. MODEL: 'Summer fun'
2. _____ : AC 490
3. _____ : 2 metres
4. _____ : 4 metres
5. _____ : 50 c.m.
6. _____ : P.V.C.

B.

Article: _____

7. _____ : 1.7 litres
8. _____ : 2.0/2.4 kw
9. _____ : 220/240 V.
10. _____ : Use a damp cloth / No detergent
11. _____ : Do **not** overfill.

C.

Article: _____

12. _____ : Full size / International standards
13. _____ : Folds in half
14. _____ : Plastic cover available
15. _____ : 12 months
16. _____ : Free of charge (allow 14 days)

D.

Article: _____

17. _____ : 32
18. _____ : Beige
19. _____ : Angora 60% / Pure new wool 40%
20. _____ : V. neck
21. _____ : [40°]

model   size   capacity   voltage   guarantee   material   accessories
depth   washing instructions   style   storage   reference number
colour   warning   dimensions   cleaning   composition   consumption
delivery   diameter (large size)   diameter (small size)

© Deirdre Howard-Williams and Cynthia Herd 1994
HEINEMANN ENGLISH LANGUAGE TEACHING

Festivals and Feast Days

What do you know about these English festivals and feast-days?
Put a ☒ next to the correct answer.

For example:

1. *Guy Fawkes' Day* is
   a always on November 5th. ☒
   b when you eat turkey. ☐
   c in mid-summer. ☐
   d to celebrate independence. ☐

2. *Boxing Day* is
   a on 26th December. ☐
   b on 2nd January. ☐
   c different each year. ☐
   d once a month. ☐

3. *New Year's Day* is
   a a public holiday. ☐
   b only celebrated in Scotland. ☐
   c an ordinary working day. ☐
   d a holiday only for schools. ☐

4. *Easter* is
   a on the same day every year. ☐
   b when you eat pancakes. ☐
   c always in April. ☐
   d when you eat chocolate eggs. ☐

5. *Christmas* is
   a always on Sunday. ☐
   b when you make good resolutions. ☐
   c when you have a decorated tree. ☐
   d when you eat a leg of lamb. ☐

6. *Good Friday* is
   a the Friday before Christmas. ☐
   b the Friday before Easter. ☐
   c when you give presents. ☐
   d to celebrate the Queen's birthday. ☐

7. *A Bank Holiday* is
   a only celebrated in Wales. ☐
   b only a holiday for people who work in banks. ☐
   c when the Queen gives money to the poor. ☐
   d a public holiday. ☐

8. *Mother's Day* is
   a always on a Saturday. ☐
   b when mothers give presents. ☐
   c when mothers get presents. ☐
   d always in May. ☐

9. *St. Valentine's Day* is
   a to celebrate the patron saint of England. ☐
   b when you send romantic cards to those you love. ☐
   c a public holiday. ☐
   d the shortest day of the year. ☐

10. *A leap year* is
    a when the year ends in 0 (eg 1990). ☐
    b every 5 years. ☐
    c a year with 366 days. ☐
    d when there is a new king or queen. ☐

© Deirdre Howard-Williams and Cynthia Herd 1994
HEINEMANN ENGLISH LANGUAGE TEACHING

Body Talk

All these compounds begin with a part of the body. Can you complete them?

For example:

1. BACK *bone*
2. BACK
3. BACK
4. HEAD
5.
6.
7. FOOT
8.
9.
10. HAIR
11.
12.
13. HAND
14.
15.
16. EYE
17.
18.

Odd One OUT 4

Here are 8 groups of words, all connected with the countryside.
Which word is the odd one out in each group?

For example:

1. (bridge) fence hedge wall

2. plough spade meadow rake

3. shed gate hut farmhouse

4. crops hens leaves seeds

5. rabbit pig goat bee

6. cliff pool pond well

7. road way path field

8. corn hay bush wheat

VERB PIECES

A lot of English verbs are made of 2 parts, a verb and a preposition. Look at the pictures and then choose the correct parts from A and B to describe them.

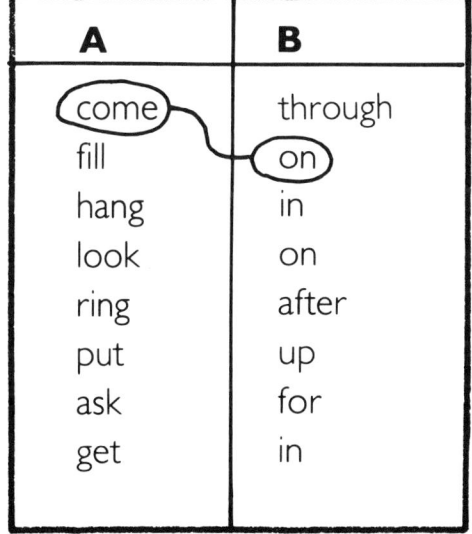

For example: 1. Come on.

A	B
come	through
fill	on
hang	in
look	on
ring	after
put	up
ask	for
get	in

© Deirdre Howard-Williams and Cynthia Herd 1994
HEINEMANN ENGLISH LANGUAGE TEACHING

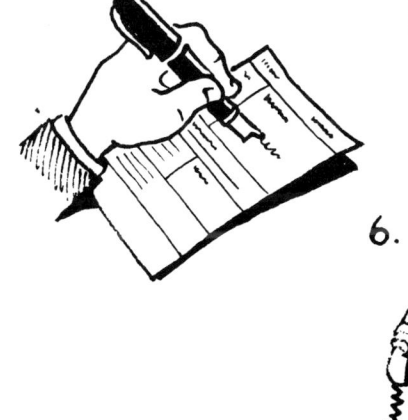

Answers

OO and EE
Page 6
OO: boot, wool, roof, cooker, root, balloon, pool, moon, scooter, door, floor
EE: queen, feet, tree, wheel, sheep, fifteen, sleeve, knee

Masculine & Feminine
Page 7
Feminine: 1. female 2. actress 3. aunt 4. cow 5. stewardess 6. queen 7. heroine
Masculine: 8. lion 9. Englishman 10. master 11. husband 12. waiter 13. nephew 14. gentleman

Clothes
Page 8
1. a large handkerchief
2. a plain T-shirt
3. a patterned bra
4. a short-sleeved sweater
5. a child's raincoat
6. a silk tie
7. a plastic belt
8. a collarless shirt
9. a dark suit
10. fur gloves

Odd One Out 1
Page 9
1. listen
2. team
3. string
4. beef
5. meaning
6. roof

Money
Page 10

price, cheque, cash, discount, coin, tax, tip, earn, cost, bill, salary, receipt, wage, profit, currency

At the Theatre
Page 11
1. cloakroom
2. booking office
3. bar
4. entrance
5. ladies
6. gents
7. emergency exit
8. back seats
9. row
10. front seats
11. orchestra
12. stage
13. curtain

What Would You Say?
Page 12
1. What's the matter?
2. Sorry.
3. How do you do?
4. Excuse me.
5. No thank you.
6. Good luck.
7. That's a pity.
8. Cheers.
9. Mind out!
10. What a surprise!
11. May I introduce you to Peter Brown.
12. Cheerio.

Abbreviations
Page 13

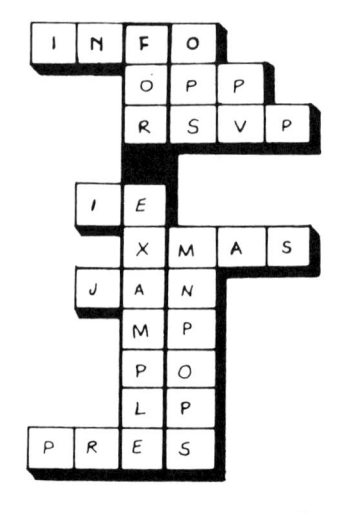

For Example = e.g.

Emergency
Page 14
1. A vet
2. E police
3. H ambulance
4. C fire service
5. F electrician
6. B dry cleaner
7. D mechanic
8. G optician

Crossword 1

Page 15

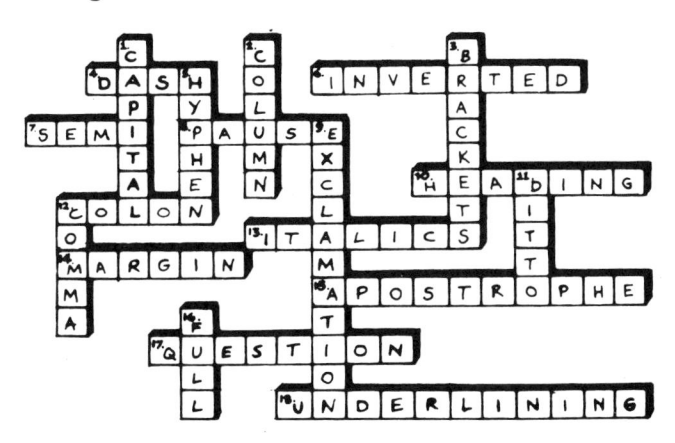

(Crossword solution with answers: DASH, INVERTED, SEMI, PAUSE, COLON, HEADING, ITALICS, MARGIN, APOSTROPHE, QUESTION, UNDERLINING)

Christmas Shopping

Page 16

Christmas list: spade – Bill   teddy bear – Liz   fridge – Sue   shirt – Jim   shoes – Mary   pack of cards – Dick   record – Mike   purse – Kate   suitcase – Joe   hammer – Bob   cupboard – Anne   football – Tom   Christmas cake – Jane

Super Shop departments: Children's – teddy bear   Do-it-yourself – hammer   Food – Christmas cake   Footwear – shoes   Furniture – cupboard   Games – pack of cards   Gardening – spade   Kitchen – fridge   Luggage – suitcase   Men's – shirt   Music – record   Sports – football   Women's Leather Goods – purse

Prepositions 1

Page 18

1. at university
2. at home
3. at peace
4. at war
5. at work
6. at breakfast
7. at church
8. at full speed
9. at school
10. at sea

Person or Thing?

Page 19

Person: driver, passenger, photographer, player, employer, traveller, foreigner, labourer, member, grocer, interviewer, dancer, farmer

Thing: lighter, saucer, cooker, shower, scooter, typewriter, notepaper

Nationalities

Page 20

(Word search grid)

Chinese   Indian   Egyptian
British   Dutch   Mexican
Russian   French   Scottish
American   Austrian   Spanish

Word Families

Page 21

1. Atlantic, Mediterranean, Pacific, North Sea
2. electricity, phone, water, gas
3. rock, classical, pop, jazz
4. buffet, snack bar, canteen, pub
5. Australasia, Africa, Europe, Asia

Thieves

Page 22

1. hedge, drainpipe, television aerial, window
2. dustbin, bricks, washing line, ladder
3. clock, handbag, picture, jewellery
4. torch, footprints, blood, scarf

Help in the Home

Page 23

1. Please fill the kettle.
2. Please feed the dog.
3. Please repair the vase.
4. Please lay the table.
5. Please fasten the dress.
6. Please polish the desk.
7. Please change the sheets.
8. Please post the letter.
9. Please cook the sausages.
10. Please carry the bag.
11. Please paint the cupboard.
12. Please wrap the book.
13. Please clean the carpet.

Make a Choice

Page 24

1. b 2. b 3. a 4. b 5. a 6. b 7. a 8. b 9. b 10. a

Shopping Centre

Page 25

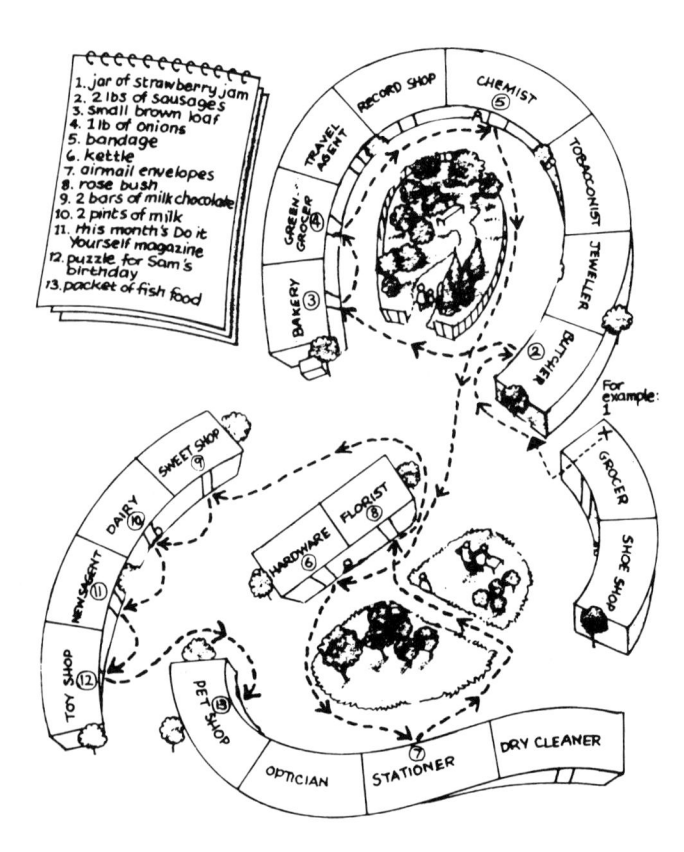

Doubles 1

Page 26

central heating, record-player, Prime Minister, information desk, snack bar, driving licence, bus stop, crossroads, letter box, car park, washing machine, petrol station

Thank You

Page 27

1. Thank you for the visit.
2. Thank you for the present.
3. Thank you for the meal.
4. Thank you for the help.
5. Thank you for the call.
6. Thank you for the advice.
7. Thank you for the lift.
8. Thank you for the party.
9. Thank you for the loan.
10. Thank you for the hospitality.

Work for Us

Page 28

Head of Languages in private school:
full responsibility, high salary, long holidays, generous pension

Car factory needs workers:
friendly colleagues, free transport, short hours, self-service canteen

Private secretary for travel agent:
pleasant boss, electric typewriter, modern office, travel opportunities

Odd One Out 2

Page 29

1. beer
2. get up
3. cabaret
4. waiter
5. course
6. 20th century

Prepositions 2

Page 30

1. in love
2. in bed
3. in tears
4. in ink
5. in danger
6. in half
7. in town
8. in pieces
9. in prison
10. in a hurry
11. in trouble
12. in turn

Travel Quiz

Page 31

1. b 2. c 3. b 4. c 5. c 6. c 7. a 8. a 9. b 10. d 11. a 12. c

Where Does It Go?

Page 32

1. A plant goes in a flower pot.
2. Tobacco goes in a pipe.
3. A sleeping bag goes in a rucksack.
4. An evening dress goes in a wardrobe.
5. A pound note goes in a wallet.
6. A purse goes in a handbag.
7. A document goes in a brief case.
8. A rose goes in a vase.
9. A saw goes in a tool box.
10. Rubbish goes in a wastepaper basket.
11. Water goes in a bucket.
12. A monkey goes in a cage.

Crossword 2

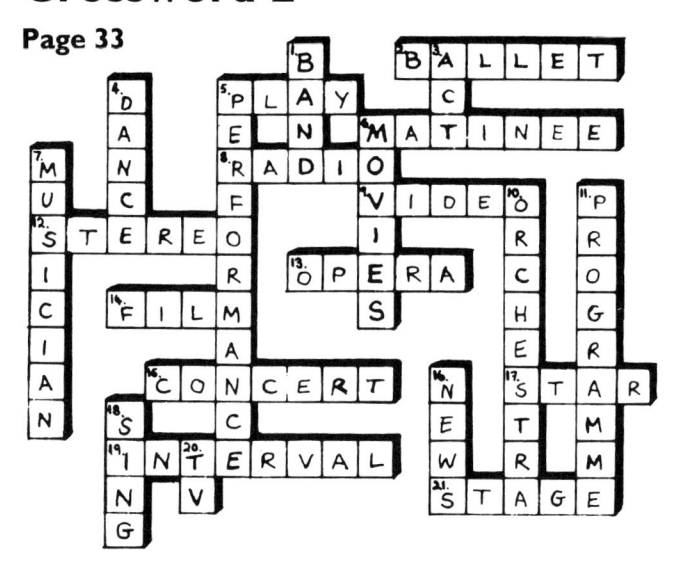

Page 33

Prefixes and Suffixes

Page 34

1. useless
2. lioness
3. self-service
4. spoonful
5. Japanese
6. non-iron
7. mini-skirt
8. rebuild
9. changeable
10. leader
11. hairy
12. unusual

In the Press

Page 35

Contents	Page
Careers Information	2
Entertainments Guide	4
Births, Marriages & Deaths	4
Travel & Holidays	6
TV & Radio	7
Readers' Letters	9
Foreign News	10
Business	12
Advertisements	12
Sport	13
Horoscopes	14

Books

Page 36

1. He is studying poetry.
2. He is studying wine-making.
3. She is studying psychology.
4. He is studying computer science.
5. She is studying antiques.
6. He is studying jazz appreciation.
7. She is studying keep fit.
8. She is studying dressmaking.
9. He is studying the modern novel.
10. She is studying translation.
11. He is studying first aid.
12. She is studying banking.

The Word Snake

Page 37

fares, ship, platform, motorcycle, leave, engine, east, traffic, connection, on board, departure, reservations, steward, driver, roundabout, ticket, terminal, luggage, get off, far, return, near, arrival, liner, railway station, north, hire a car, road, deck, kilometres, stop, port of embarkation

Time Off

Page 38

1. parasol, swimsuit, deck-chair, suntan lotion
2. material, needle, tape measure, thread
3. rod, hook, net, line
4. plaster, wallpaper, tiles, paste
5. compass, climbing boots, stick, rope
6. push-chair, nappies, cot, talcum powder

The Word Snail

Page 39

farm, market, tractor, orchard, donkey, yard, ditch, harvest, stream, mill, lamb, berries, sheep, plants, soil, log, grass, signpost, tool, leaves, straw, waggon, nest, tree, earth, hen, nuts, stones, shed, hedges

Words Easily Confused

Page 40

1. price
2. channel
3. hotel
4. teacher
5. audience
6. surgeon
7. attendant
8. mistake
9. bank
10. fees
11. voyage
12. bath
13. newspaper
14. fence
15. duty
16. housework

Doubles 2

Page 41

1. boarding pass
2. left-handed
3. earring
4. youth hostel
5. secondary school
6. second-hand
7. lampshade
8. news bulletin
9. false teeth
10. timetable
11. evening class
12. opening hours
13. home-made
14. service charge
15. thunderstorm

Words Beginning With CAR-

Page 42
1. caravan
2. careful
3. carrot
4. cardigan
5. cart
6. carriage
7. carpenter
8. caramel
9. cargo
10. card
11. Caribbean
12. carpet

Odd One Out 3

Page 43
1. reduced
2. tiny
3. ugly
4. slow
5. sad
6. spotless
7. bold
8. sickly

Make and Do

Page 44
1. make progress
2. make faces
3. do the housework
4. make a cake
5. do the gardening
6. make a choice
7. make a speech
8. make friends
9. make trouble
10. make an effort
11. make a film
12. do the shopping
13. do business
14. do the washing-up
15. make a joke
16. do one's/your homework

Words and Meanings

Page 45
1. book
2. bank
3. leaf
4. train
5. note
6. stick
7. park
8. band
9. sink
10. tap
11. plane
12. change
13. box
14. plant
15. mark
16. record
17. post
18. saw
19. race
20. hand
21. jam

The Wastepaper Basket

Page 46
1. a label
2. a cheque
3. an application form
4. a telephone message
5. a letter
6. a timetable
7. a ticket
8. a telex
9. a guarantee
10. a bill
11. a memo
12. an invitation
13. an advertisement
14. an order form
15. a receipt

The Name Game

Page 47
1. Step**hen**
2. **Pet**er
3. **Anth**ony
4. **Ja**mes
5. **Mat**thew
6. Phi**lip**
7. **Rich**ard
8. **Rob**ert
9. Har**old**
10. Er**nest**
11. Pa**trick**
12. Mar**tin**
13. Ali**son**
14. **Car**oline
15. **Wen**dy
16. **Rose**mary
17. **Ra**chel
18. **Sand**ra
19. **Jan**et
20. **Jan**ice

Cross It Out

Page 48
1. windscreen, brake
2. pink, purple
3. accountant, architect
4. Catholicism, Judaism
5. ring, coin
6. Jupiter, Mars
7. Suez, Panama
8. fees, rent
9. ankle, chin
10. slides, prints
11. Socialism, Communism
12. honey, nuts
13. guitar, violin
14. shorts, scarf
15. doorway, ceiling

The word left is **puzzle**.

What's On The Menu

Page 49

Starters: prawn cocktail, chilled melon, soup of the day, avocado pear
Fish: fresh Dover sole, fried plaice with parsley sauce, grilled mackerel, seafood pie
Meat: steak and kidney pie, roast beef and Yorkshire pudding, baked ham and pineapple, Madras chicken curry
Vegetables: brussels sprouts, new potatoes, plain boiled rice, creamed cauliflower
Desserts: lemon meringue pie, chocolate mousse, fruit salad with cream, cheesecake
Drinks: red house wine (by the glass), real English ale, fruit juices, minerals

Connections

Page 50

The 2 missing letters are:
1. LE
2. CE
3. ME
4. OW
5. VE
6. ER
7. CH
8. TE
9. NE/TE
10. RE
11. DE
12. EF
13. AR
14. IN
15. SH
16. SA
17. ST
18. AT
19. KE
20. AL

The Family Tree

Page 51

1. Sidney is Steve's grandfather.
2. May is Steve's grandmother.
3. John is Steve's grandfather.
4. Alice is Steve's grandmother.
5. Ray is Steve's uncle.
6. Vera is Steve's aunt.
7. Alan is Steve's step-father.
8. Ruth is Steve's mother.
9. Roger is Steve's father.
10. Christopher is Steve's father-in-law.
11. Doris is Steve's mother-in-law.
12. Nancy is Steve's cousin.
13. Ann is Steve's sister-in-law.
14. Dave is Steve's brother.
15. Mary is Steve's first wife.
16. Pam is Steve's second wife.
17. Adam is Steve's nephew.
18. Irene is Steve's niece.
19. June is Steve's daughter-in-law.
20. Eric is Steve's son.
21. Joy is Steve's daughter.
22. Wendy is Steve's step-daughter.
23. Tracey is Steve's granddaughter.

Words Ending in -TION

Page 52

1. reservation
2. qualification
3. question
4. competition
5. direction
6. collection
7. translation
8. operation
9. exhibition
10. pollution
11. population
12. revolution

The S Connection

Page 53

trousers, scissors, shorts, tights, pyjamas, glasses, crossroads, news, customs, mathematics, stairs, clothes, jeans

Collectives

Page 54

1. staff
2. flock
3. class
4. crowd
5. committee
6. club
7. jury
8. fleet
9. bunch
10. audience
11. queue
12. collection
13. orchestra
14. team
15. union
16. crew

Complaints

Page 55

1. It's melted.
2. It's broken.
3. It's dusty.
4. It's stretched.
5. It's blunt.
6. It's bad.
7. It's overripe.
8. It's dirty.
9. It's leaking.
10. It's torn.
11. It's scratched.
12. It's loose.
13. It's cracked.
14. It's bent.
15. It's slow.

Language Functions

Page 56

1. F
2. C
3. N
4. H
5. I
6. E
7. M
8. K
9. L
10. P
11. D
12. B
13. T
14. S
15. A
16. R
17. Q
18. J
19. O
20. G

Proverbs

Page 58

1. A stitch in time saves nine.
2. A bird in the hand is worth two in the bush.
3. An Englishman's home is his castle.
4. Many hands make light work.
5. Half a loaf is better than none/no bread.
6. One man's meat is another man's poison.
7. You can lead a horse to water but you cannot make him drink.
8. People in glass houses should not throw stones.

Doubles 3

Page 59

1. charter flight
2. bypass
3. waterproof
4. office worker
5. dishwasher
6. toenails
7. boarding school
8. opera house
9. notepaper
10. sightseeing
11. baby-sitter
12. native language

The Weather Forecast
Page 60

frost
shade
sunshine
mild
gale
icy
freeze
lightning
heat
overcast
warm
mist
storm
damp
shower

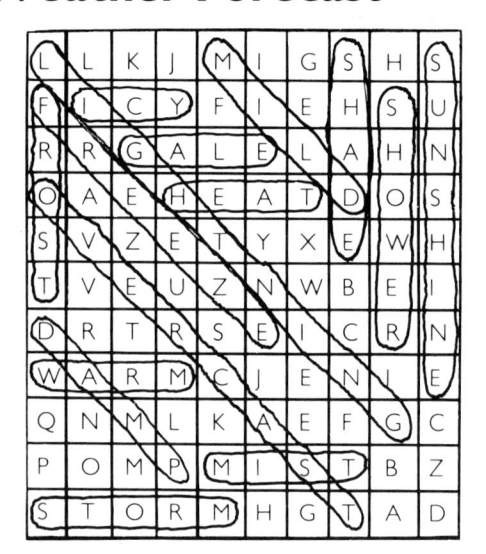

Purchases
Page 61

A Children's pool:
1. model 2. reference number 3. diameter (small size) 4. diameter (large size) 5. depth 6. material

B Electric kettle:
7. capacity 8. consumption 9. voltage 10. cleaning 11. warning

C Table tennis table:
12. dimensions 13. storage 14. accessories 15. guarantee 16. delivery

D Sweater:
17. size 18. colour 19. composition 20. style 21. washing instructions

Festivals and Feast Days
Page 62

1. a 2. a 3. a 4. d 5. c 6. b 7. d 8. c 9. b 10. c

Body Talk
Page 63

1. backbone
2. backyard
3. backache
4. headmaster
5. headquarters
6. headlines
7. footprints
8. footsteps
9. footpath
10. hairdresser
11. hairbrush
12. hairdryer
13. handwriting
14. handbag
15. handshake
16. eyelid
17. eyelash
18. eyebrow

Odd One Out 4
Page 64

1. bridge
2. meadow
3. gate
4. hens
5. bee
6. cliff
7. field
8. bush

Verb Pieces
Page 65

1. come on
2. put through
3. look after
4. ask for
5. ring up
6. hang on
7. fill in
8. get in

Word List

The numbers beside each word are the page numbers where the word is used in a game. If the word is used often, you will see the first three page numbers followed by ...

A

abbreviation 13
abroad 31
accessories 61
accountant 48
ache 47
act 33
actor 7
actress 7
address 46
adjective 43
advertisement 28, 35, 46
advice 27, 57
aerial 22
Africa 21
after 47
against 54
age 46
air 31
airmail 25
album 50
ale 49
all 36
allow 61
alter 45
always 62
ambulance 14
American 20
amusement 31
angora 61
ankle 48
another 52, 58, 59
answer (n) 38
ant 47
antique 36
apology 56
apostrophe 15
application form 46
appreciation 36
April 62
architect 48
area 45
army 50
arrival 37
arrive 52
article 61
Asia 21
ask for 65
assistant 40
Atlantic 21
atom 50
attendant 40
au pair 23
audience 40, 54
aunt 7, 51
Australasia 21
Austrian 20
available 61
avocado 49
awful 57

B

baby(ies) 24, 38
baby-sitter 59
back 11
backache 63
backbone 63
backyard 63
bad 55
bag 23
baked (adj) 49
baker 25
ballet 33
balloon 6
band (music) 45, 33
band 45
bandage 25
Bank Holiday 62
bank (money) 45, 47, 62
bank (of river) 40, 45
banking 36
bar (café) 11
bar (chocolate) 25
basement 9
basket 46
bath 40
bathe 40
bathroom 38
beach 38
bean 47
bed 30
bee 64
beef 9, 49
beer 29
before 62
begin (begun) 42, 63
beige 61
belief 48
below 49
belt 8
bent 55
berry(ies) 39
best 44
better 56, 58
bill 10, 29, 31 ...
bird 58
birth 35
birthday 25, 62
block 45
blood 22, 29
blunt 55
board (on board) 37
boarding pass 41
boarding school 59
body 26, 45, 48
boiled (adj) 49
bold 43
book (n) 23, 24, 36
book (v) 45, 59
booking office 11
boot 6
boss 28
bottle 24
bottom 47
box (v) 45
box 29, 42, 45
Boxing Day 62
boy 24
bra 8
brackets 15
brake 48
bread 58
break (broken) 14, 55
breakdown (broken down) 14
breakfast 18
breath 50
brick 22
bridge 64
briefcase 32
British 20
brother 51
brown 25
brussel sprouts 49
bucket 32, 57
buffet 21
build 56
bull 7
bunch 54
bus stop 26
bush 25, 38, 58 ...
business 35, 44
busy 46, 56
butcher 25
buy (bought) 25, 55
bypass 59

C

cabaret 29
cage 32
cake 16, 44
call 27
can (n) 58
canal 40, 48
candle 50
canteen 21, 28, 46

capacity 61
capital (letter) 15
car 14, 28, 45 ...
car park 26
caramel 42
caravan 31, 42
card(s) 16, 42, 62
cardigan 42
care 59
career 35
careful 42, 57
carefully 36
cargo 42
Caribbean 42
carpenter 42
carpet 23, 42
carriage 42
carrot 42
carry 23
cart 42
cash 10
castle 58
Catholicism 48
cauliflower 49
ceiling 48
celebrate 62
cellar 9
cement 50
centimetre (cm) 61
central heating 26
century 29
certainty 57
change 23, 45
changeable 36
charge 31, 46, 61
charter flight 59
cheek 50
cheerful 43
cheerio 12
cheers 12
cheesecake 49
chemist 25
cheque 8, 46
chicken 49
child 8
children 17, 31, 46
chilled 49
chin 48
Chinese 20
chocolate (milk chocolate) 25, 49, 62
choice 24, 44
choose 31
Christmas (Xmas) 13, 16, 29 ...
church 18
circle 45
class 31, 54
classical (music) 21
clean 23
cleaning 61
clever 56
cliff 64
climbing boots 38
cloakroom 11
clock 22, 36
cloth 61
clothes 8, 54

club 54
clue 47, 48, 53 ...
cm (centimetre) 61
coal 50
coat 41
coffee 24
coin 10, 48, 50
collarless 8
colleague 28
collection 52, 54
collective 54
college 36, 40
colon 15
colour 48, 61
column 15, 41, 59
come on 65
comma 15
committee 54
common 30
Communism 48
compass 38
competition 52
complain 55
complaint 55, 56
complement 57
complete 49, 63
composition 61
compound (adj) 41, 59
compound (n) 63
computer 36
concert 33
confuse (confused) 40
connect (connected) 39, 60, 64
connection 37, 50, 53
consumption 51
contact 46
container 45
contents 35
cook 23
cooker 19
corn 64
correct 40, 54, 65
correctly 44
cost 10
costly 43
cot 38
could 57
country(ies) 31
countryside 39, 64
course 29
cousin 51
cover 61
cow 7, 24
cowardly 43
crack (cracked) 55
cream 49
creamed 49
crew 54
criticism 56
crops 64
cross (v) 48
cross out 48
crossroads 26, 53
crossword 15, 35
crowd 54
cupboard 16, 23

currency 10, 31
curry 49
curtain 11, 38
customs 53
cut(v) 45

D

dairy 25
damage 22
damp 60, 61
dance 33
dancer 19
danger 30
dark 8
dash 15
data processing 36
daughter 51
daughter-in-law 51
day 61, 62
dear (expensive) 43
death 35
deck 37
deck-chair 38
declare 53
decorate (decorated) 62
delivery 61
department 17
departure 37
depth 61
describe 8, 41, 44 ...
description 8, 46
desk 23
dessert 49
detergent 61
devil 50
diameter 61
dictionary 36
die (died) 51
different 9, 38, 45 ...
difficult 20
dimension 61
dinner 41
direction 52
dirty 14, 55
discount 10
dish 50
dishwasher 59
ditch 39
ditto 15
divorce (divorced) 51
do 44
do-it-yourself (DIY) 17, 25
doctor 40
document 31, 32
dog 23, 24
donkey 39
door 6
doorway 48
double 6, 25, 41 ...
doubt 56
Dover sole 49
down 14
drainpipe 22
dress 14, 23
dressmaking 36

drink (n) 49
drink (v) 58
driver 19, 37
driving licence 26
dry cleaner 14, 25
dustbin 22
dusty 43, 55
Dutch 20
duty 40

E

e.g. (for example) 13
each 41, 48, 54
earn 10, 36
earring 41
earth 39
easily 40
east 37
Easter 29, 62
eat 48, 62
effort 44, 48
egg 62
election 52
electric 61
electrician 14
electricity 21
emergency 14
emergency exit 11
employer 19
end (n) 47
end (v) 52, 62
enemy 50
engine 37
engineer 42
England 62
English 36, 39, 41 ...
Englishman 7, 58
Englishwoman 7
enormous 43
enough 57
enquiries 53
entertainments 35
entrance 11, 46
envelopes 25
error 50
Europe 21, 31
evening class 41
evening dress 32
every 47, 62
everyday 12
example 13, 38, 39 ...
exclamation mark 15
excuse me 12
exercises 36
exhibition 31, 52
experience 42
explanation 31, 57
express 56
expression 30
extra 31
eye 45
eyebrow 63
eyelash 63
eyelid 63

F

face(s) 44
factory 28, 45, 56
fail 29
false teeth 41
family (ies) 52
family tree 51
fare 31, 37
farm 39
farmer 19, 24
farmhouse 64
fasten 23
father 51
father-in-law 51
fault 40
favourite 56
feast 62
fee 40, 48
feed 23
feet 6
female 7
feminine(f) 7
fence 40, 64
festival 62
field 9, 64
fifteen 6
fight (v) 45
fill in 28, 47, 61 ...
film 33, 44
finally 48
find 22, 29, 30 ...
finish 50
fire 14
fire service 14
first 50, 51
first aid 36
fish 25, 49
fishing 38
fit (adj) 43
fit (v) 57
fix 45
flame 50
flat 45
fleet 54
flight 31, 59
flock 54
floor 6
florist 25
flower pot 32
fold (v) 61
following 25
food 17, 25, 31
football 16
footpath 63
footprint(s) 22, 63
footstep 63
footwear 17
for example (e.g.) 13
forecast 60
foreign 31, 35
foreigner 19
form (v) 59
form 31, 46
free 28

free of charge 46, 61
freeze 60
French 20, 36, 41
fresh 49
fridge 16
fried 49
friend (friendly) 28, 31, 44
frightened 43
front 11
frontier 31
frost 60
fruit 45
fruit juice 49
fruit salad 49
full 18, 28, 58
full stop 15
fun 61
functions 57
fur 8
furniture 17

G

gale 60
gallery 29
game(s) 10, 17, 47
gardening 17, 44
gas 21
generous 28
gentleman 7
gents 11
geography 41
get 31, 37, 62
get in 64
get off 29
get up 29
girl 23, 47
give 10, 45, 49 ...
glad 43
glass(es) 14, 21, 24 ...
gloves 8, 45
glue 45
go down 45
goat 64
Good Friday 62
good 57, 62
good luck 12
goods 17
graceful 43
granddaughter 51
grandfather 51
grandmother 51
grapes 36
grass 39
gratitude 56
green 45
greengrocer 25
greeting 31
grilled 49
grocer 19, 25
ground 9, 45
group 9, 21, 43 ...
grow 45
guarantee 46, 61
guest 31

guide 35
guitar 48
Guy Fawkes 62

H

hairbrush 32, 63
hairdresser 63
hairdryer 63
hairy 34
half 30, 58, 61
ham 49
hammer 16
hand (n) 45, 58
hand (v) 45
handbag 32, 63
handkerchief 8
handshake 63
handsome 43
handwriting 63
hang on 65
happily 47
hardware 25
harvest 39
hat 20
hay 64
head (boss) 28
heading 15
headline 63
headmaster 63
headquarters 63
health 59
healthy 43
heat 60
hedge 22, 39, 40 …
help (n) 23, 27, 52 …
help (v) 10, 14, 42 …
hen 39, 47, 64
Her Majesty's (HM) 40
here 36, 52
hero 7
heroine 7
high 28
hire (hire a car) 37
history 41
hit (v) 45
HM (Her Majesty's) 40
holidays 28, 31, 35
home 18, 23
home-made 41
homework 40, 44
honey 48
hook 38
horoscope 35
horse 9, 58
hospitality 27
hostel 40
hotel 25, 31, 40
hour(s) 28, 57
house 23, 58
house wine 49
housework 40, 44
how do you do? 12
huge 43
hurry 30
husband 7

hut 64
hyphen 15

I

i.e. (in other words) 13
ice 47
icy 60
identify 20
ill 14, 47
immediately 57
immense 43
immigration 31
incorrect 9
independence 62
index 50
Indian 20
information (info) 13, 26
ink 30
instruction 61
instrument (music) 48
insurance 31
international 61
interval 33
interviewer 19
introduce 12
inverted commas 15
invitation 46
iron (non-iron) 34
italics 15
items 35

J

jam (traffic) 45
jam 25, 41, 45
January (Jan) 13
Japanese 34
jar 25
jazz 21, 36
jeans 53
jewellers 25
jewellery 22
Job Centre 42
job 28, 48
joke 44
journey 31, 40
Judaism 48
Jupiter 48
jury 54
just 48

K

keep fit 36
kettle 23, 25, 50 …
kidney 49
kilometre 37
kilowatt (kw) 61
kind 31, 48
king 7, 62
kiss 9
kitchen 17
knee 6
knot 58

know 62
kw (kilowatt) 61

L

label 46, 61
labourer 19
ladder 22, 29
lady (ies) 7, 11, 41
lamb 39, 62
lamp 14
lampshade 41
land (v) 45
language 28, 56, 59
large 8, 61
lavatory 9
lay 23
lb (pound) 25
lead 58
leader 34, 38, 40
leaf (leaves) 39, 45, 64
leaf (paper) 45
leap year 62
leather 17
leave 25, 31, 45
left-handed 41
leg 14, 62
lemon meringue pie 49
less 53
letter (alphabet) 42, 50, 52 …
letter 23, 35, 45
letter box 26
library 36
lie 31
lift 26
light (adj) 58, 62
light (music) 21
light (v) 64
lighter 19
lightly 45
lightning 60
like (v) 56
likes (n) 56
line 38
liner 37
lion 7
lioness 7, 34
lip 47
list 8, 16
listen 9
litre 61
live 31, 47
loaf 25, 58
loan 27
log 39
long 28
long-playing record (LP) 13
look after 38, 65
look at 51, 53, 56 …
look out 57
loose (adj) 55
lot 52, 65
lotion 38
love 30, 62
LP (long-playing record) 13
luggage 25

luncheon vouchers 49
LV (luncheon vouchers) 49

M

mackerel 49
Madras curry 49
magazine 8, 25, 40
make 24, 38, 41 …
male (m) 7
man (men) 47, 56, 57 …
many 58
margin 15
marital status 46
mark (n) 45
market 39
marriage 35
married 51
Mars 48
masculine 7
master 7
mat 47
match(es) 24, 54
matchbox 24
material 38, 45, 61
mathematics (maths) 41, 53
matinee 33
matter(s) 10, 12
meadow 64
meal 25, 27
meaning 9, 45, 50
meat 49, 58
mechanic 14
Mediterranean 21
melon 49
melt (melted) 55
Member of Parliament (MP) 13
member 19, 52
memo 46
mend 57
menu 49
meringue 49
merry 43
message 31, 46
metre 61
Mexican 20
mid-summer 62
mild 60
milk 25
mill 39
million 47
mind (v) (mind out) 12
mind 36
mineral (drink) 49
miniskirt 34
missing 28
mist 60
mistake 8, 40, 44
mistress 7
model 61
modern 28, 36
money 10, 14, 45 …
monkey 32
month 25, 46, 61
more 53, 57
mother 24, 51

Mother's Day 62
mother-in-law 51
motorcycle 37
mountain (Mt) 38
mousse 49
movies 30, 33
museum 29
music 17, 45
musician 33

N

name (n) 8, 42, 46 …
name (v) 8
nappy (ies) 38
nation 45
nationality (ies) 20
native language 59
near 37
neck 61
need 38
nephew 7, 51
nest 39, 47, 50
net 38, 39
New Year's Day 29, 62
new 61
new potatoes 49
news 31, 33, 35 …
news bulletin 41
newsagent 25
newspaper 35, 40
niece 7, 38, 51
nine 58
no thank you 12
nobody 45
non-scheduled 59
none 50
North Sea 21
north 37
note (money) 45, 50, 56 …
note (music) 45
note (v) 45
notepaper 19, 48
noun 53, 54
novel 36
number 25, 42, 52 …
nut 39, 48

O

object 31
occupation 46
odd 9, 29, 43 …
off 38
offer 56
office 28, 46
office worker 59
oh dear! 56
old 47
on board 37
once 62
onions 25
only 52, 53, 62 …
opening hours 41
opera 33
opera house 59

operation 52
opinion 57
opportunity 28
opposite (opp.) 13
optician 14, 25
orange 55
orchard 39
orchestra 11, 33, 54
order (n) 34, 57
order form 46
ordinary 62
out 9, 29, 43 …
outside 31
overcast 60
overfill 61
overripe 55
own 31, 59
owner 50
oxygen 50

P

Pacific 21
pack (of cards) 16
packet 25
page 8, 35, 45 …
paint 23
pair 40
pancake 62
paper 45, 46
parasol 38
parcel 31
park (v) 45
park 31, 45
parsley sauce 49
part 26, 45, 47 …
particular 37
party 27
pass 29
passenger 19
passport 53
paste 38
path 64
patron saint 62
patterned 8
pause 15
pay 31, 48
payment 31
PE (physical education) 41
peace 18
pear 50
pension 28
people 14, 38, 54 …
performance 33
period 46
permission 57
person 19, 45
pet 14, 47
pet shop 25
petrol station 26
phone 21
photograph 48
photographer 29
picture 6, 22, 40 …
pie 49
piece(s) 31, 45, 46 …

pig 9, 64
pillar 45
pineapple 49
pink 48
pint 25
pipe 32
pity 12
place 31, 45, 54
plaice 49
plain 8, 45, 49
plan 38
plane 45
planet 48
plant (factory) 45
plant 32, 45, 49
plaster 38
plastic 8, 46, 61
platform 37
play (n) 33
play (v) 45, 56
player 19
pleasant 28
please 46, 57
plough 64
plural 53
plural-form 53
poem 36
poetry 36
point (n) 45
poison 58
police 14
polish 23
political 48
pollution 52
pond 64
pool 6, 61, 64
poor (adj) 57
pop (music) 21
population 52
port (of embarkation) 37
Post Office (PO) 13
post (n) 45
post (v) 23, 45
potato(es) 49
pound (lb) 25
pound note 32
prawn cocktail 49
preferences 56
prefix 34
present (n) 16, 27, 62
President (Pres.) 13
press 35
pretty 43
price 10, 31, 40 …
primary school 41
Prime Minister (PM) 26
print (photography) 48
prison 30
private 28
prize 40
problem 14
professor 40
profit 10
programme 33
progress 44
proverb 58

psychology 36
pub 21
public 62
public house 41
punctuation 15
purchase 61
pure 61
purple 48
purse 16, 32
push-chair 38
put 31, 41, 45 …
put on 29
put through 65
puzzle 25, 48
PVC 61
pyjamas 53

Q

qualification 51
queen 6, 7, 62
question 22, 52
question mark 15
queue (n) 54
quite 20
quiz 31

R

rabbit 64
race (n) 45
race (v) 45
radio 33, 35
rail 45
railway 37
railway station 37
raincoat 8
rake 64
rapid 43
razor 9
read 36, 48
reader 35
real ale 49
rebuild 34
receipt 10, 31, 46
receive 46
recognise 46
recommend 31
record (n) 16, 31, 45
record (v) 31, 45
record shop 25
record-player 26
red 49
redecorate 38
reduced 43, 59
reduction 31
reference number 61
relation 50, 51
religion 48
remember 45
rent 48
repair (n) 46
repair 23
reply (RSVP) 13
request 56
reservation 37, 52

reserve(d) 45
resolution 62
responsibility 28
rest (n) 56
retirement 59
return 37
revolution 52
rice 49, 50
rich 47
ring 48
ring up 65
ripe 55
river 45
road 37, 64
roast beef 49
rob 47
rod 38
romantic 62
roof 9, 57
room (n) 48
room (space) (n) 57
root 6
rope 38
rose 25, 32, 47
round 48
roundabout 37
row 11
RSVP (please reply) 13
rubbish 32
rucksack 32
run 45
Russian 20
rusty 43

S

sad 43
safe (adj) 45
Saint 62
salary 10, 28, 40
sale(s) 44, 52
same 62
sand 47
saucer 19, 50
sausage 23, 25
save 36, 46, 58
saw (n) 32, 45
saw (v) (past of see) 45
scared 43
scarf 22, 48
school 18, 28, 45
science 36
scissors 53
scooter 6, 19
Scotland 62
Scottish 20
scratch 55
sculpture 24
sea 18, 31
seafood pie 49
seat 11, 41, 50
second 50, 51
second-hand 41
secondary (school) 41
secretary 28
see 31, 45

seed 64
self-service 28, 34
semi-colon 15
send 62
service 14
service charge 29, 41
sewing 36
shade 60
shadow 50
shed 39, 64
sheep 9, 39
sheet 23
shell 50
shelter 50
ship 37
shirt 8, 16
shoe 16, 25
shop 25
shopping 17, 25, 44
shopping centre 25
shopping list 25
shore 40
short (shortest) 28, 62
short-sleeved 8
shorts 48, 53
should 56
show 47
shower 19, 60
sickly 43
side 45, 50
sightseeing 59
sign (n) 45
signpost 39
silk 8
sing 33
single 31
sink (n) 45
sink (v) 45
sister-in-law 51
sit 31
situation 12, 27
size 61
skirt (miniskirt) 34
sleeping bag 32
slide 48
slow 43, 55
small 25, 51
smaller 56
smile 9
snack 31
snack bar 21, 26
snail 39
snake 50
soap 9
socialism 48
soil 39
solution 14
some 53
someone 56
something 31, 55
son 24, 47, 51
sorry 12, 56
sound (adj) 43
sound (n) 45
soup of the day 49
South America 42

spade 16, 64
Spanish 20
speak 59
spectators 40
speech 44
speed 18
speedy 43
spoonful 34
sport 17, 35
spotless 43
square 45, 50, 60
St Valentine's Day 62
stadium 9
staff 54
stage 11, 33
stained 43
stairs 53
standard (n) 61
star (person) 33
start 50
starter(s) 49
stationers 25
stay 31
steak and kidney pie 49
step-daughter 51
step-father 51
stereo 33
steward 7, 37
stewardess 7
stick (n) 38, 45
stick (stuck) 45
stitch 58
stone 39, 58
stop 37, 63
storage 61
storm 60
straw 39
strawberry 25, 29
stream 39
stretch (stretched) 55
strike 63
string 9, 50
strip (n) 45
student 36
study 36
style 61
subject 36
subtitle 52
suffix 34
sugar 45
suggestion 56
suit 8
suitcase 16
sum (money) 46
summer 61
sunshine 60
suntan 38
super 17
sure 56, 57
surface 45
surgeon 40
surprise 12, 56
sweater 8, 61
sweet (n) 25
sweet shop 25
swift (adj) 43

swimsuit 38
sympathy 56

T

T-shirt 8
table 23, 41, 52 ...
table tennis 61
take (n) 44
take (took) (v) 46
take off 29, 45
talcum powder 38
talk 23, 63
tap (n) 45
tap (v) 45, 57
tape 45
tape measure 38
taste 9, 31
tax 10, 40
teach 45
teacher 40
team 9, 54, 56
tear (torn) (v) 55
tears 30
teddy bear 16, 17
telephone (v) 49
telephone message 46
television aerial 22
telex 46
tell 36
term 40
terminal 37
test 29, 50
thank you 12, 27, 56
theatre 11, 29
thief (thieves) 22, 50
thing 19, 48, 54 ...
think 57
thirst 50
those 62
thread 38
throw 58
thumb 50
thunderstorm 41
ticket 31, 37, 46
tie 8
tights 53
tile 38
time 38, 46, 48
timetable 41, 46
tin 47
tiny 43
tip 10, 29
title 36
tobacco 32
tobacconist 25
toenail 59
together 32
tomato 29
tonight 59
tool 39
tool box 32
torch 22, 50
towel 9
town 30
toy 25

tractor 39
traffic 37, 45
train (v) 45
train 31, 45, 52
translation 36, 52
transport 28
travel 28, 31, 35
travel agent 25, 28
traveller 19
tree 39, 45, 62
trick 47
trip 31
trouble 30, 44
trousers 53
try 44, 56
try on 29
turkey 62
turn 30
TV (television) 33, 35
two 58
typewriter 19, 28

U

ugly 43
uncle 7, 51
underlining 15
unemployment 59
union 54
university (Univ.) 18, 41
unreasonable 43
unusual 34
us 28
use 22, 31, 34 …
useless 34

V

V-neck 61
vase 23, 32
vast 50
vegetable 49
verb 65
verse 50
vet 14
video 33
view 25
violin 48
visa 31, 50
visit 27
voltage 61
vote 52
voyage 40

W

wage 10
waggon 39
wait 31
waiter 7, 29
waitress 7
Wales 62
walk 38, 45
wall 64
wallet 32
wallpaper 38

want 42
wanted 28
war 18
wardrobe 32
warm 60
warning 31, 57, 61
wash up 45
washing 61
washing line 22
washing machine 26
washing-up 44
wastepaper basket 32, 46
water 21, 32, 45 …
waterproof 59
wave 50
way 25, 50, 64
wear 31, 48
weather 60
wedding 60
weekend 38
welcome 31
well (adj) 56
well (n) 64
well-known 58
what's the matter? 12
wheat 64
wheel 6
whether 44
which 43
wife 7, 51
win (won) 45, 47
window 22, 57
windscreen 48
wine 24, 49
wine-making 36
woman (women) 17, 24
woodwork 41
wool 6, 61
word 39, 40, 41 …
work 14, 18, 28 …
workers 28
working (adj) 62
worth 58
wound 36
wow! 56
wrap 23
write 51, 58
writing 15
wrong 9, 54, 55

X

Xmas (Christmas) 13

Y

yard 39
year 62
Yorkshire pudding 49
young 31
youth hostel 31, 41